mo+th

Issue Number Four
+FALL 2006

Los Angeles Poets & Writers Collective

Bombshelter Press
+ LOS ANGELES

mo+th

Issue Number Four

Fall 2006

Editor: Vicki Whicker

Series Editor: Jack Grapes

Layout & Design: Alan Berman

Cover Design & Digital Art: Ellen Jantzen

ISBN 0-941017-79-6

mo+th is published by Bombshelter Press. Contributing authors are members of the Los Angeles Poets & Writers Collective, which sponsors writing workshops, readings, seminars, retreats, and literary publications including *ONTHEBUS*, *Wednesday*, and mo+th. We do not accept unsolicited submissions. Subscriptions and general correspondence should be sent to Bombshelter Press, P.O. Box 481266, Bicentennial Station, Los Angeles CA 90048. Single copies of mo+th can be ordered for $15.00 plus $1.50 shipping. A subscription for four issues costs $50 (postpaid).

info@bombshelterpress.com

www.bombshelterpress.com

Los Angeles Poets & Writers Collective

www.jackgrapes.com

con+tents

FELLOW CREATIVE BEINGS, an hour or so ago, each of you made the decision to come here. To step into the apocalyptic heat and humidity, to step into your cars to make your way through the mad rush, to step through that door and sit here in this book-lined space. Know that your decision today has made the world an even more magnificent place.

BUT I KNOW THAT HERE IN THIS CITY, a city where luck, fate, talent and non-talent can create a biohazard, a city where smiles, money, sex, and greed boil in a frenzy, producing chemical reactions in which it's hard to trust the strength of the bonds, a city where you can be made or broken in the same day, here, amidst all this, we, you, the artists have survived. And we must keep going.

I ASK YOU TO JOIN ME in a call for courage for you, for me, and for every creative soul.

A tragedy occurs every day when someone gives up, when the channels are stopped, when a piece of art is killed before its time.

You may have stopped something beautiful midway,

You may have stopped something ugly midway, not knowing that it is beautiful,

You may have stopped something ugly midway, not rejoicing in its ugliness,

You may have stopped because the eyes around you did not see you, could not see you, didn't want to see you,

You may have stopped because the critic's eye within you tore you down, made you ashamed, suffocated your creative spirit,

You may have stopped because someone asked you what you "do" for the fifty millionth time and you were finally too tired, too worn down, too frustrated to explain.

I ask you: Please don't stop what you do. Don't stop, don't stop, don't stop, keep going until you lose track of time.

I speak from a place of privilege—I've had schooling that has given me armor for the world, that has allowed me to explore, that almost made my parents go broke, I have a roof, I have food, I have love in my life. All this has given me strength and support to pursue what know I need to pursue. But even so, I find it hard to keep going. You may have faced the same. So this prayer is for all of us, no matter what our position in life, a prayer to keep creativity alive.

So I pray that you keep going, you who hold the pen, you who hold the paintbrush, you who hold the script as you step on stage, you, you, you, you know who you are, you must hold your own like the flowers that grow out of cement cracks. We must have the diamond-cut courage to go on, to not let the machinery of this world, the traffic, the white smiles, the orange tans, the thin starved muscles, the excesses, the wants, the extravaganzas, the veneers make us question what we do. Stand with me and plant your feet deep into this land, this tar pit orange tree desert shrubbed ground, stand in the tar pit with the old bones and scream, *I'm not going anywhere!*

Because of our work, the world is stronger,
Because of our work, the world will go on and mend,
Because of our work people might be able to stand next to each other and respect each other's gods,
Because we believe, the world will believe,
Because we believe, future generations will have something real to hold onto, to look back on, to inspire new work.

We all must travel onward bringing our light, our jewels, our incense, our nonsense, our sixth sense to the world, lighting up the dark caverns of the brain, showing people who they are, and who they can be.
We let people look at themselves in a new light, let people see each other again for the first time, look in the mirror and see a new life, a new possibility, a new way of living, a new hope, a new love for someone or something.
Sometimes we wander through the smog, the fog, the clogged streets, smelling exhaust, smelling of exhaustion, covered in the sweat of another job we may not want to do. But we must believe in that feeling we all know. The feeling you get when the sweat is pouring from your heart because of the excitement, the excitement that makes our hearts thunder, that makes the walls quake, that speaks to everyone.
We are warriors, we are wizards, we are the messengers of the gods, we must do it, we must communicate, we must keep the channels open, to let the ocean of creativity flow, flow, flow into and out of us, we are the hunters and gatherers of the soul, we must keep going, keep going, keep going, if you fall, we will be there to pick you up, but YOU must keep going, until you can't anymore.
And then keep going.

This is my life: cooking. I cook my own food every day. I eat vegetables, some certain grains, and a few other things. About four times a year I go out to a restaurant because the types of oils even in healthy restaurants don't agree with me. I have food sensitivities. This limits my social life and my mobility, not to mention it takes a lot of time to cook my every meal and clean it up. I remember when I was really sick, how I would splurge on pizza. Then I got to a place where I would track it. It would usually take me about a week to ten days to recover from a slice, having to go to a doctor or even catching a cold just from the disruption.

I feel like I have learned to keep a lot of secrets. I mean, most people do not eat like me. Nor do they really understand the prices I have to pay when I go off my diet.

So, when people ask me about my diet, sometimes I just don't know where to start because it really is a whole story to tell, a way of life. So, I have learned to do a few things to hide it, or play it down, or change the conversation because I am just not in the mood to educate others. Maybe I'm not in the mood to be the odd one out, to receive that look of disbelief, and worse, to hear their line of questioning into my own real understanding of my body.

I guess I have learned to suss people out. I read their intentions pretty quickly because I have other parts of my life that are as central to me as wearing clothes, that require a conversation or an education, or perhaps a whole story. Like, I have gay parents. Yes, that could be considered another secret. Found out at ten when they got divorced. And some years later, after getting through the 'My-dad-is-gay story,' and, 'No, kissing him does not give me AIDS,' the plot thickens as my mom, unflinchingly straight, starts seeing a woman.

So, maybe I don't dream the American dream. I can't eat the American food. And I don't really have the American family. Sure, intellectually it is one thing. But what does it do to the young girl I was? Not only did I go through puberty and the questions it brings, I also had larger questions like, 'What is sexuality?' Without someone handing sexuality to me on a platter, defined, at least somewhat defined, I had to reinvent the wheel and discover it for myself. This has its plusses and minuses. On one hand, I appreciate the kind of cellular questioning I got to go through because it has made sexuality and the gender roles that seem to so readily accompany it my own. Not someone else's. Though the minuses are there too, like how I feel like a late bloomer. Now in my thirties, I'm dating, and sometimes tripping over gaps in my knowledge, stumbling, stupid and hopefully endearing as my date's face crinkles or squirms.

Still, it is my life. And I am more content with it than I ever have been. I remember as a kid thinking to myself that I could be anywhere, in any country, with parents of different cultures. What does it matter what other kids think? Are they not just by-products of their culture? There are so many varieties of life. I felt this truth in my body at eleven, developed it, and leaned on it, and maybe it's where I was when some of the other kids were playing kissing games.

I was nineteen when the fatigue came. It hit me like a drowning one day. I did not come up for air until years later. And then years after that, once I had reshaped my psyche, did I begin to understand what I'd lived through. It came one afternoon. My eyelids shut like a cellar door and my muscles gave way. I remember my arms instinctually bracing me, rigid, as I hit the white couch pillow. The pillow was made in an intentionally imperfect fabric, as was the style. My mom always had the new styles. I sunk. We had just gone to a Buddhist temple for Mother's Day, our first time to this kind of worship. And the images of the Buddhist monks began to swirl with my less-conscious thoughts of a painted stairwell and of the cannister of Coke on the window sill. Fever. Proportion between the waking world and sleeping one was lost. And I was lost, like being shipwrecked with water all around, but no sign of the life and the body I knew.

It lasted from nineteen years old till about 27 or 28. Calling it first Mono, then Chronic Fatigue Syndrome. It's another secret I keep.

Like the one I keep when asked, "Where did you go to college?" I don't always want to tell the story that I didn't have the strength to walk down the hall to shower. Or that I used the money my parents saved for me to attend college, to live on. And the money went quickly, with no earnings coming in, and doctor bills to pay. And I don't say that I couldn't live at home during this time. That actually, living with either of my parents made my condition worse. And really, trying to live at home was like putting a bomb-shelled soldier right back into the battlefield. My closest friends didn't get it. "Why can't you just go home for a while?" they'd ask directly, or more so, indirectly. But this was my truth at nineteen. Another secret revealed that, for me, family equaled stress, overwhelming stress.

Now here at 34, it is the first time that I can fully financially support myself without going into debt. I feel like I am pulling back another layer of what fell into the couch that day. Here I am, somewhat normal. Somewhat similar to my peers. And what I feel is a deeper understanding of the pressure I have felt to catch up. To survive. To meet those basic needs of life; they are such an accomplishment to me. Me, who was one of the top in my class. My system starts to exhale.

I used to think that the illness made me special. Or better. Or worse. But more so now, I feel, well, this is my life, this is my experience. It is not better or worse than anyone else's. It is.

And I have waited the strength in me. I have waited to patiently try to tell some of my secrets. Not because they are all that special. But because they are a part of me. And it is me that I want. It is life I want: embarrassing, terrifying, thrilling, and real.

And there is timing to life, and this is my time to speak.

Libby Barnes + ***One Point Off***

In elementary school, we had a Gifted and Talented program and I took the test to be included. I don't know if I was picked by the teachers to take it or if my parents insisted. I think the teachers probably picked me since I was in the smart classes most of the time. The only part I remember was a page with a bunch of circles on it and I was instructed to make the circles into pictures of anything I wanted.

To this day, every once in a while, I think about what I should have done with those circles to show that I am, in fact, Gifted and Talented. I should have done unusual things—some small, some big. Not anything ordinary like turning two circles into tires of a car or connecting them to make a caterpillar. But thinking very small—like making one a molecule and then doing something very big or strangely abstract. Of course, right now I can't think of anything really genius, so I'm sure they were right that I'm not, in fact, Gifted and Talented.

When the results came back, sure enough, I was not accepted into the program. If memory serves me, the principal of my school, Mr. Slonaker, a very nice man, told my parents that I missed it by one point. I was one point off from being, in fact, Gifted and Talented. I guess that was supposed to make someone feel better—to know that I'm really close, but just not quite enough.

I don't recall being particularly upset, but I do remember sometimes seeing Jana and Eric, two kids who were, in fact, Gifted and Talented, getting to do special tasks at a special table and wishing I could, too. My parents were very protective, so I'm sure they made it clear to me that my school was dumb and the test was dumb and they didn't know what they were talking about. But I do still think sometimes about those circles and what I could have done to be more clever.

That was in fourth grade; and, the next year, my parents pulled all of us, my brother, sister and me, out of public school and into private school. Not in protest of the Gifted and Talented debacle, but because my brother got teased for always raising his hand in class. He's very smart. I wonder if he was in the Gifted and Talented program? I don't actually know. I don't think my sister was. She's smart, too, but in more of a practical way, not a Gifted and Talented way.

And I'm just one point off.

Barbara Bartels + ***The Smell of Childhood***

The sun is everywhere, the air calm
The chlorine smell from the pool
I breathe deeply to take in the eucalyptus
Freshly mowed grass scent fills the air

Roses and honeysuckle wafting through
The open window
Mint of toothpaste getting brushed
On little teeth

The Ivory soap of clean and ironed clothes
Breakfast being prepared, bacon frying
Coffee brewing
Breakfast odors can be dense
We're too excited to eat

Mother's hair, soft, smells of Avon's lemon shampoo
She likes to sniff my forearm
It reminds her of sweet milk
Now I sniff my arm all the time

Sigrid Bergie + ***February 15***

Today Tony and I stood in our bathrobes singing "Happy Birthday" to my mother Marga over the phone. She was pleased—she said we sounded like a barbershop quartet, the two of us.

Tony left Marga and me to talk. Mainly we talked about my father. I call him Vati—that's German for Daddy. He's 88 years old and can barely walk. My 82-year-old, nearly blind mother takes care of him—and I visit them regularly to help out.

She tells me he is worse—he is not interested in anything, not in eating, not in talking—he doesn't read anymore. He dreams a lot and when he is awake he sees people and animals (we do not see) in the apartment. Napoleon I and Josephine are recent guests. I don't know if they are spirits or what.

My father's thinking isn't as straight and he does all kinds of screwy things to drive my mother (and me) crazy. She tells me she prays to be more patient—that it makes one stronger. Frankly I think Mother Teresa would lose patience with my father.

I asked Marga if she got her birthday package. She said, "No, not yet, but I'm not thinking about my birthday. Your father doesn't even know it's my birthday."

I knew she wasn't looking for sympathy. I knew her mind was mainly on surviving each day, each hour, and each minute. But I knew there was something I needed to do for all of us.

So I said, "Put Vati on, if he's not sleeping."

I hear Vati's voice in my receiver, "Hello, Sigrid. How are you?" I ask him how he is and tell him I'm looking forward to visiting him in a few days.

Then I ask him, "Do you know today's date?"

His voice fades, "Is it, ahh, February 21st?"

I answer, "No, it is February 15th."

There is a silence on his end. I ask him, "Do you know who was born on February 15th?" I repeat, "Do you know who was born on February 15th?"

There is no answer. But I can feel my father thinking. Is it possible to feel someone thinking through the phone from Minnesota to California?

I even see him thinking. His soft blue eyes are alert and his thick silky white hair that needs a cut, frames his still-handsome face. His now too-thin body wears plaid lounge pants and black dress shoes, with no shirt and no socks.

I see the high ceilings of my parents' downtown apartment and the snow drifting on the sidewalk and street four stories below. I see the round black table by Romeo's chair—and the two brownish ceramic coffee cups sitting side by side and never empty, thanks to Marga's magic hands.

I sense the exquisite animal presence of my mother on her phone—listening, really listening with brain and heart and coal-black eyes.

I feel my father is about to give birth to an answer, though I don't know what it is—or maybe his thoughts will just drift away like the blowing Minnesota snow to another place and there will be no answer.

I wait in our house on the hill, at my long white panel desk. Outside my window, the big old pine tree reaches his straggly arms out to comfort me.

And then I hear it—the steady slow rumble of my father's voice.

He answers, "It's a birthday. It's Marga's birthday."

Leslie Berliant + ***First Blood***

We take up space in the middle of
the sidewalk, like entitled children playing in the street,
disinterested in anyone's irritation or amusement.
40 is the new 16, after all.
Nervous, I hear him say, temporarily deaf as a fish.
I'm nervous, too, I say.
Yes, you, you're trembling. The Cheshire Cat smiles,
starting to evaporate.
I kiss him harder, want to
bite his bottom lip,
draw first blood and make him mine.
My calves don't want to hold me up,
weak as peony stems from a
rush of chlorophyll to
deeper, greedier parts.
Car door unlocks
and locks again, judgmental as
my mother.
The click, click warning me to go.
But graceful exits require
complex choreography, steps
I can't remember.
I am deaf and dumb.
I run my hand over the Clash T-shirt,
feel a hard swimmer's body hiding
underneath, like a stealth soldier,
seeming benign, but ready to attack at
any provocation.
Hands like roving minstrels
move from down
the back of my skirt to each
side of my face. Our foreheads
touch. My lungs ache from
this peak air. I am dizzy, high
as an acrobat and distracted with thoughts
of a Clash concert when I was a real 16
and a nameless boy's sweaty hands were
down the front of my pants, searching
for a quickening pulse.
He had magician's hands to make me
feel beautiful and ashamed, right there

in the Aragon Ballroom, barely concealed
behind the speakers. But without the weight
of names, we were
revelers at a masked ball.
Hidden and free.
Now I am called out. I am fresh kill,
gutted and splayed open
for everyone on this Venice sidewalk.
I throw my hands around those oak branch
arms. Push myself against that compact
body as his cock locks onto me. Through
layers of cloth and regret,
I will myself to stop shaking.

Leslie Berliant + *I Dreamed about Your Feet Last Night*

I dreamed about your feet last night.
They were long and elegant,
not small and square as a box
of crayons, like mine.
You called the little blocks
I walk on 'Picasso feet'.
I imagined your earlobes coming towards me,
icy as snow drifts,
slippery like drizzle slicks.
I dreamed that my forehead was pressed against
your kneecap. That you kissed my left pinky
over and over again,
sending me thought bubbles
in the dishwater.
I dreamed that you asked me to tell you
my secrets. Asked me to remove my appendix and make
room for you. Asked me if I would
love you for a while, maybe longer.
I dreamed that you asked me to know you,
know your family,
know your regret,
know your broken downness,
your discontent,
your self-immolation.

I wanted to sing yes, oh yes, I will
puncture a lung for you, give you all my
breath as a keepsake. I will open my throat
wide enough to swallow your bones,
your sorrow,
your restlessness,
your disease.
But sometimes in dreams
I lose my voice, just as when I am awake
and near you. I am fluster and flush
and a crimson breastplate.
I dreamed you said you could
love me if I cracked my walnut shell for you
and gave you the soft, bitter nut
to chew.
I dreamed you called me your whore
and cried for my innocence. When you came,
you spoke God's ineffable name and like an alchemist,
you changed me from tin to gold.
I dreamed you said you could love me
if I would believe you could love me.
If I howled for you
and undressed for you
and lay my intestine on the ground for you
and let you into
my untamed world.

Alan Berman + *Villanelle*

We drive too fast, too easy to give in
to forces strong that draw with constant praise.
To crush the things we love, an easy sin.

I step to counter impulse, loss's win,
and find it patient, waiting out my days—
we drive too fast, too easy to give in.

To survey hopes, our hearts must be open
despite the cautions that reflexes raise:
to crush the things we love, an easy sin.

I glimpse the rear-view mirror to begin—
can't be distracted by tedious delays—
we drive too fast, too easy to give in.

Our lapses vary, canceling the din
of compromise, the calculated phrase;
to crush the things we love, an easy sin.

Accepting flaws: constant obligation
to move, to pause; I learn the several ways
we drive too fast, too easy to give in
to crush the things we love, an easy sin.

Linda Blakeley + ***Reckoning***

Tall buildings sway in the desert, hiding secrets a thousand years old.
Twisted ropes, tied in knots, hang from the tallest trees.
Clocks tick, without hands, marking time.
Clothes sit in baskets waiting to be hung up to dry.
Mothers drink coffee, tapping their feet, songs on the radio.
Babies wait in their cribs, no milk to fill empty stomachs.
Angry fathers refuse to change diapers.
Wives on strike demand their Bill of Rights.
The headless horse draws the Ace of Spades from the deck.
The number eight teases the cow jumping over the moon.
The rooster crows at 4:30 in the morning easter time.
Death comes to all who wait in line.
Dance down new paths,
Discover new roads.
March through Central Park to the zoo where lions and tigers roar.
Monkeys, hanging from branches, scratch themselves.
Snakes slither in their cages.
The keeper calls out, "Only one snack before dinnertime."
His keys jingle as he turns the lock.

Adrian Bloom **+ *Death to the Ego***

When I make the final exit,
I can't look back
and say I didn't try
to expand, to grow,
to break through barriers;
even if it was to no avail;
there must be something noble
about that,
even if it just meant
bloodying the skull
while banging the head.

John Brocato and Josh Grapes + ***The Scottish Play***

Chapter one: freshly ironed irony

"Simplicity is absurd, and absurdity is genius. A true genius is something simple. This chorus-line opening is not deep, but overdone. I failed to make something deep happen. I failed to make emotion happen. I failed to make thought happen. I'm stuck somewhere in between thought and emotion."

He continues speaking with comedic seriousness.

"It's almost something."

He belches, and speaks the next cliché in a monotone voice.

"Never give up."

He looks down in frustration. I'm stuck somewhere between four other people.

"Although I seem to be incapable of depth, I tend to nail irony."

How is this ironic? I'm not sure.

"This is not absurd, this is not deep genius, this is not deep thought."

I'm not trying to make absurdity happen, though I'm pretty sure this is absurd. We need nothing more, not even something deep.

"I am stuck between Andy Warhol and the primitive man."

Whatever that means. I tell the story of a world—not the world, as I hope it's not the one you know, but a world. I also tell the story of mathematics not ruling this world. I tell the story of a person who despises math, yet feels it has a purpose. I tell the story of Picasso-type people who do nothing but measure blood flowing from a dead woman's body. I tell the story of a director who cares about a world that no one else even bothers to recognize.

"I tell the story of a joke."

Chapter two: death of a bad pun

"OK," I said. "Take two." My actor, who had just finished the monologue that starts off this book—or whatever this is—spoke.

"Do I have to say this whole thing again?"

I took this opportunity to say something again, safe in the shelter of quotation marks.

"Well, of course. You can't get it right until you know what you're doing. You can become what you want to become in life. You can eventually be good at what you read."

"But you don't know what I read. What I read is what you just said. I said 'Never give up.' You said 'Follow your dreams!' Well, you know what? Last night I dreamt I dug a big hole! But worst of all is all these people who walk around doing nothing but walk around so quickly it's like their life depends on it! But 6 plus 2 is still 8. And that's why I'm a confused actor, sir!"

I listened to him, and thought about what he had said. Then again, I had to listen to what he said, and think about it. I'm a director. Slash-writer. It's what I'm paid to do. It isn't much, but pay's not why I'm in this business. I'm in this business because I was written into this business. Slash-directed. So, like I said. I thought. I thought very hard, even though very says nothing when you add it to a sentence. It's like when I repeated thought. It puts emphasis. But it does nothing.

Oh, I get it now! It does nothing. Just like people. That was my actor's argument. And he was right. He was so right.

Six plus two does equal eight.

Unfortunately, thought plus thought only equals two different thoughts. There is no omnipotent combination. There is no holy matrimony between the thoughts. There's only another idea to lose sleep over.

"All right, people."

This is me speaking again. If you couldn't tell. Does this sound like an actor to you, after all? Do I have my sweatshirt thrown over my right shoulder, bought cheap and never actually worn? Do I clasp my hands together, raise them over my head, and thank a god I don't believe in after every show? Well, enough existential writing only meant to fill up the page.

"It's time to get back to work. Let's start from the top."

But I believe in it. I'm a director. Slash-writer. Slash-character. Sans everything.

Chapter Three: absurdity at its most mediocre

Sans everything, by the way? That's Shakespeare. And that right there? That was me showing off. But back to business. Seeing as we slash-me slash-I slash-us are slash-is directing a play, this chapter is going to be written like a—guess for me? I am the director, after all. You have to listen to me. You listen to God, after all. And he slash-she slash-it is a director. And God doesn't even talk to you directly. God doesn't even get a paycheck. So this is going to be written—just for this chapter, and maybe another one or two—like a fucking play. All right? Good (maybe).

(The stage is completely white, two chairs on opposite sides of the stage. One table downstage. Table covered with cans and bottles.)

GUMBOIL: I found her outside, lying in a pool of sound and fury signifying a systemic change in the anomaly of our solitary, poor, nasty, brutish, and short peach trees!

NAPTIME: Ye gods, man!

GUMBOIL: That's what your mom said tomorrow!

(Enter PELERINE from stage right. She carries the body of a WOMAN bleeding from the mouth—one can use blood capsules, or fake blood—and is dressed in a purple spandex jumpsuit and neon green angel wings, and has a big foam hand with "Number 12" on her actual hand. The hand may be blue, if desired)

PELERINE: I picked her up, Gumboil, you shithead! All you do is talk about Hobbes-ian plantlife!

GUMBOIL: Never mind that, Pelerine! You do not even know! My mother was a binder, Pelerine! She drowned. She drowned in a sea of her own tears! A pool of sound and fury signifying a systemic change in the anomaly of our solitary, poor, nasty, brutish, and short peach trees!

PELERINE: You're getting repetitive like in nature to an oft-molested ear fracture! This is evidenced in page 219 in a book no one bothers to read, when Maypop says to Phosgene, "That is not Queen Elizabeth III, that is my wife!" But this problem is bigger than us and the postal system. We have got a bleeding lady. Naptime, fetch Prostate. We have got a woman to save!

NAPTIME: I wish I had more lines!

(NAPTIME exits through the audience and returns with PROSTATE, who wheels in a cart filled with medical supplies—real medical supplies are needed. PROSTATE puts the WOMAN on the table, carefully taking off the cans and bottles, then pushes her off to make room for the medical supplies so that she lays among the broken bottles and crushed cans)

PROSTATE: Naptime filled me in on what we have to do. So let us proselytize. Naptime! Ruler!

(NAPTIME hands PROSTATE a ruler)

DIRECTOR: Wait, stop. What if the characters had normal names, like Timothy, or Philip, or Frederic?

NAPTIME: This play is stupid.

DIRECTOR: I'm the director.

NAPTIME: Sorry.

DIRECTOR: Take it from the top!

(The ACTORS groan in unison)

DIRECTOR: All right. From where we left off. But with the normal-slash-brilliant names this time.

BOB: Okay, we have got the ruler. Now when?

TOM: Now we measure the blood, and do the rest of the things we must do as so thoroughly detailed in the Holy Bible.

(BOB, TOM, PERRY, the WOMAN and SAM all laugh heartily at this joke. Tom ends up explaining it to the others)

TOM: Part One. Scene 3-and-a-half-teen.

SAM: What you mean, of course, is that it is your imperative to euthanasia, the pillow prison.

TOM: Verily!

BOB: Verily!

(Both look down in a mixture of shame, frustration, and redundancy. PERRY takes the ruler, and treating it like a holy object, begins measuring the blood that is flowing from WOMAN'S mouth. PERRY notices that the flow of blood from the left corner of her mouth is longer than the flow of blood from the right, and so dabs at it with his exposed scrotum painted with Christmas colors and adorned with Christmas lights—the phallus of Christ?—then measures the two streams of blood. DIRECTOR looks puzzled—"This is an interesting character choice," he thinks, but then is hit by REALIZATION and HE WILL ADD IT TO THE PLAY. Then PERRY looks closely at the new measurements and pockets the ruler, satisfied)

PERRY: Seventeen-and-a-half inches, sir or madam.

(WOMAN's eyes gleam with tears of joy, and her words are spoken with the utmost truth, love, and sincerity)

WOMAN: Thank you.

(WOMAN expires. DIRECTOR continues typing slash-writing his thoughts that seem to function as a narrative—no, they DO function as a narrative—in this book, if you could call it

that. His thoughts read, "The play worked out well, if not strangely. Then again, 'strange' is the heart of the absurd, as I assume continuing to write in the italicized, and possibly circumcised, parentheses that are customary to blocking or written direction in a play slash-screenplay when the play section of this book is over-dash-for-dramatic-emphasis-for now. I am surprised by the depth of understanding in my actors. To be honest, I didn't understand a word. And I wrote the damn thing. Maybe they changed it? I look over my script. No. No, they didn't. The only thing they changed was adding the phallus of Christ. I liked it. It was pretty funny." DIRECTOR *looks over at his actors, who are exhausted both by a full day of hard work and the weight of their play's ridiculousness, and says, "Call it a night." The actor playing* SAM *asks* DIRECTOR *for a bigger part.* DIRECTOR *calls him a faggot.* SAM *tells* DIRECTOR *to fuck himself up the ass. All* ACTORS *leave the theater. So does* DIRECTOR. *So does* JANITOR. *So does* REALIZATION. *So does* HE WILL ADD IT TO THE PLAY.)

Chapter Four: apples to apples, dust to dust

I have to go to a party today, so I put on some cologne I bought from a homeless person outside the 7-Eleven. He asked me if I was a musician, but I said I was just a director. He looked a little sad. He looked a little disappointed. He looked a little broken, as if the world was only him and me—which is correct but doesn't sound correct—and I had taken all of his hopes and dreams and devoured them, but to a much lesser extent. I did, after all, say he looked a little broken. But he picked up the pieces, put them back together, and gave me the cologne, a pen that looked like a syringe, and a crumpled-up piece of paper with his name and number printed on it. He told me that if I ever needed a drummer to call him, and I thanked him for the offer and the stuff and went home to change into my suit I always wear slash-never wear because I don't get invited to many parties because I had to go to a party. I realized I'm beginning to write like a child, possibly because I'm subconsciously trying to sound deep. "This chorus-line opening is not deep, but overdone. I failed to make something deep happen. I failed to make emotion happen. I failed to make thought happen. I'm stuck somewhere in between thought and emotion." I copy-slash-pasted that from the first part of the first paragraph, if you couldn't tell, and I realize that I'm quoting myself, but I'm quoting my actor too. I brought the words. And he brought the feelings. I realize how sad that is, and try to pity myself, but nothing comes. I wrote it—I wrote it—and he's the one who feels it while I pretend to feel bad about myself. It's like that soliloquy from Hamlet. The only comfort I have is in my gimmick. My written slashes. I go to the party depressed, with my cheap suit, cheap cologne, cheap piece of paper with a name-slash-number written on it with a golf pencil stuck in my suit pocket as a makeshift, cheap handkerchief in an attempt to make cheap look fancy, and a glass of cheap alcohol in my left hand—the sinister hand?—and my cheap gimmick in my head.

I meet a girl at the party and she has short blonde hair and she seems interested in me. It's nice to have someone interested in me—it makes me feel special like my 1st grade teacher did when she put gold stars next to my name, maybe in a foreshadowing way, the stars of Hollywood, the stars next to my name, and makes me feel important, maybe in a selfish way—but I feel a little guilty because I know I'll never be interested in her, because I've never really been interested in anyone. This, too, is nice though. It's been a long time since I've felt anything. Maybe this party will be good for something. We keep talking, and she keeps flirting—blinking too much so that her eyelashes flutter, moving her hips suggestively, the whole schmeer—and we actually have an interesting conversation. She works for an advertising agency, and I talked about the meaning of arithmetic and my 1st grade teacher, and she looked a little bored, so I did the same old trick that works every time I pretend to be interesting: I mentioned I was a director. Slash-writer. And she forced her eyes to widen and her mouth to gape slash-smile and an excited "Oh!" to escape her throat.

"Oh!" she said, "you're a director and a writer! Are you working on anything now?"

"Yes, I am, actually. I'm putting on a play about the nature of realism. . ."

And I tell her about the play, and how much of a fag the actor playing Sam is, and she laughs, and I tell her about the phallus of Christ, and give her some satisfying bullshit about how much the play and the whole process of putting it on means to me, when really it's just something to write about slash-type about and to keep my hands busy. I fill up time. I fill up pages. I fill both with repetition. It's what I do. Sometimes I think they might all be the same thing.

She kisses me on the cheek and says I'm brilliant after we've both had too much to drink, but I push her away and she runs out of the party crying and a few of the witnesses call me an "asshole" and a "faggot." Perhaps this is my actor's revenge? I'm entertained by the thought. I admit it openly, to myself. I take out a ruler—I keep the prop in my pocket because the actors will lose it—and measure the alcohol she spilled on the hardwood floor. A circle that looks like it's perfect in the drunken stupor I'm in—3 inches in diameter—and drive home and scrape the side of my car against the curb, and measure the scrape—18 inches, not bad—and think about what she said. She said I was brilliant. So did my 1st grade teacher.

Brilliance is a concept. Nothing more.

Probably something less.

Chapter five: the absence of cod

(Opening night. The ACTORS are nervous. The DIRECTOR is not, but secretly wishes he was. The stage is completely white, two chairs on opposite sides of the stage. One table down stage. Table covered with cans, and bottles.)

BOB: I found her outside, lying in a pool of sound and fury signifying a systemic change in the anomaly in our solitary, poor, nasty, brutish, and short peach trees!

SAM: Ye gods, man!

BOB: That's what your mom said tomorrow!

(Enter PERRY from stage right. She carries the body of a WOMAN bleeding from the mouth—one can use blood capsules, or fake blood—and is dressed in a purple spandex jumpsuit and neon green angel wings, and has a big foam hand with "Number 12" on her actual hand. The hand may be blue, if desired)

PERRY: I picked her up, Bob, you shithead! All you do is talk about Hobbes-ian plantlife!

BOB: Never mind that, Perry! You do not even know! My mother was a binder, Perry! She drowned. She drowned in a sea of her own tears! A pool of sound and fury signifying a systemic change in the anomaly in our solitary, poor, nasty, brutish, and short peach trees!

PERRY: You're getting repetitive like in nature to an oft-molested ear fracture! This is evidenced in page 219 in a book no one bothers to read, when Mark says to Philip, "That is not Sally's daughter III, that is my wife!" But this problem is bigger than us and the postal system. We have got a bleeding lady. Sam, fetch John. We have got a woman to save!

SAM: I wish I had more lines!

(SAM exits through the audience and brings with him JOHN, who wheels in a cart filled with medical supplies—real medical supplies are needed. JOHN puts the WOMAN on the table, carefully taking off the cans and bottles, then pushes her off to make room for the medical supplies so that she lays among the broken bottles and crushed cans)

JOHN: Sam filled me in on what we have to do. So let us proselytize. Sam! Ruler!

(SAM gives JOHN a ruler)

BOB: Okay, we have got the ruler. Now when?

TOM: Now we measure the blood, and do the rest of the things we must do as so thoroughly detailed in the Holy Bible.

(BOB, TOM, PERRY, the WOMAN and SAM all laugh heartily at this joke. Tom ends up explaining it to the others)

TOM: Part One. Scene 3-and-a-half-teen.

SAM: What you mean, of course, that it is your imperative to euthanasia, the pillow prison.

TOM: Verily!

BOB: Verily!

(Both look down in a mixture of shame, frustration, and redundancy. PERRY takes the ruler and, treating it like a holy object, begins measuring the blood flowing from WOMAN'S mouth. PERRY notices that the flow of blood from the left corner of her mouth is longer than the flow of blood from the right, and so dabs at it with his exposed scrotum painted with Christmas colors and adorned with Christmas lights—the phallus of Christ?—then measures the two streams of blood. PERRY looks closely at the new measurements, and pockets the ruler, satisfied)

PERRY: 17 and a half inches, sir or madam.

(WOMAN's eyes gleam with tears of joy, and her words are spoken with the utmost truth, love, and sincerity)

WOMAN: Thank you.

(The ACTORS decide to add another improv. They sharpen their rulers on the medical supplies, finally finding a use for them, until they are razor-sharp, and cut into the WOMAN. WOMAN breaks character, screaming in agony. "Stop! This wasn't rehearsed! We haven't polished this yet!" but the other ACTORS pay no heed, just keep cutting and cutting, saying in unison, "We're cutting because we're cutting," until WOMAN's screams become whimpers and then they cease entirely. WOMAN expires. The ACTORS remove her perfectly-preserved organs with Broadway-type smiles, and measure them. Each one is somehow 4 inches. The DIRECTOR is shocked, and calls the POLICE, though he feels nothing. He thinks it's an interesting choice, to kill a fellow ACTOR, and watches with passive interest at the chaotic, screaming AUDIENCE trampling each other as they try to leave the theater while the actors keeping bowing and clasping their hands together, raising them over their heads to thank a GOD they don't believe in. Eventually, POLICE enter from the theater doors, downstage, to witness the ACTORS still bowing next to the body of WOMAN, who is also ACTOR, filled with adrenalin at a show well done. The POLICE take the ACTORS away and forget to question the DIRECTOR who is watching from the corner of the room. DIRECTOR gets up 18

minutes and 18 seconds after everyone has left the theater and takes out the ruler he forgot to give back to his ACTORS and begins measuring. Measuring everything.)

DIRECTOR: 7 feet, 5 inches, exactly...

WORLD: [silence]

DIRECTOR: 4 inches and 3 centimeters...

WORLD: [silence]

DIRECTOR: 1 foot, 3 inches, 2 centimeters...

WORLD: [silence]

Chapter six: nothing is funny anymore

I'm still in the theater, writing. It takes a long time to write each and every word because I have to measure each and every one. The centimeter side of the ruler has never gotten so much work. I measured everything but the words. I measured the backstage. I measured the theater. I measured the building. I measured the block. I measured the people passing by. I measured the street and the one car that stopped at a red light—which I also managed (with its post) to measure. I managed to measure the tires and the confusion on the man's face with my ruler. I measured the ruler with the ruler, I measured the thoughts going through my head, I measured the concept of brilliance, I measured the redundancy of these sentences, I measured the gimmick I use with my slashes, I measured the slashes, I measured the false-depth injected into the book, I measured realization, I measured God, I measured, I measured, measure for measure. After writing measure so many times, the word looks wrong, like it's spelled wrong, so I measure the new word, I measure measurement, and then I measure my newfound and comfortable insanity. I get in the car after measuring it like I measured the confused man's car and just keep driving, taping the ruler to the back of the car near the exhaust pipe so I could measure the streets I was driving down, but forgot to measure the tape which keeps gnawing the back of my brain, but I can't stop driving, I can't stop measuring the street. I can't stop for people, they are dying for a reason. I will stop driving when I feel like it or my ruler breaks, and then I will cry because my ruler is broken and I don't know where to get another one, and then I will cry harder because I can't measure my sadness and I can't measure the hopelessness of not being able to buy another ruler. Then I will think about it. I will think about all of it, I will think about measuring it, and I will measure the thought, and think about the measurement, and measure that thought too. I realize that my life is a joke. Everyone's life is a joke. Life itself is a joke. And death? Death is the punchline.

Chapter seven: knife, library and the happiness of pursuit

(HOLLY sits on the chair, and the lights are off, except for the light in the kitchen. She waits for her husband, HAL, tears dried on her cheeks, betrayal mixed with love in her eyes. The door opens, and in comes HAL, stage right.)

HOLLY: Where have you been?

HAL: Out.

HOLLY: I know you were just at the slut's house, fucking her.

HAL: Yeah? Well that's because our relationship's gone to shit!

HOLLY: I'm sorry! It's my fault...it's all my fault...

(HOLLY begins to cry again, HAL's anger subsides and turns to love intermingled with sadness)

HAL: No, Holly...I'm sorry. The fault is mine. But we can start over. We can make it all better.

HOLLY: I love you.

HAL: I love you too.

(HAL and HOLLY move to the couch and become comfortable in each other's arms like a fetus in its mother's womb, and watch the sunset. DIRECTOR sits in his chair, and with his index finger—he has calculated its length, mentally—measures the armrest. Blackout.)

Chapter eight: dadaism

;

Laura Caputo + ***The In-Between Space***

I have to be honest
or I want to be
in saying that
I hate this place,
this space in between.
It's not black.
It's not white.
It's various shades of grey
and my stomach is nervous,
like I could vomit
vomit up my anxiety,
my pain,
my fears of not knowing
and yet,
I stay.
Committed to finding out
what I'm so scared of,
waiting for the chatter
of right and wrong
to die down,
hoping that somewhere
beyond all this confusion
and through all of this storminess
I will be standing strong
in fearlessness
being every ounce of divinity
they tell me I contain.
And still it lingers
lasting for hours
and minutes
and centuries
and days.
This pain—
it teaches me
the very lesson
I said I've wanted to learn.
It keeps me close
to the moment
sometimes deep inside of it,
like now...
and I can hear my insides

crying outside.
I'm giving voice
to the space in between.
In between
thoughts and tears
between
head and feet
between
body and heaven
and right now
I must stay
here
and now
without reason,
without answer,
without purpose.
Stay...staaaayy...stay!
Oh, puppy one
I have to be honest
or I want to be
and this staying in the middle
this floating with no life preserver
this falling with no ground in sight
is the hardest thing
I've ever had to do.

Celia Chapman + ***Gabrielina***

I never wondered about the statue before.
Veiled by her fountain, her shimmering curtain of water and light,
she graces the intersection of two angled streets at the far edge of the city.

The woman kneels quietly,
contemplating what fallen soldier, belonging to what vanquished god?
Around her: a small courtyard, benches, flowering vines trailing green leaves
like careless hands stroking the faded walls.

No one walks in this neighborhood.
They only travel in cars,
the road too far from the kneeling statue to make out who she is.
Behind her a slash of green cordons her off from the houses and the incurious eyes
of those who live there.

Surely someone knows her name.
Knows why she was chosen to stand guard at this corner of the city.
Knows why this corner, and no other.

But she is silent behind her veils of water, dappled with shadow and light,
the patterns of shadow and light the only expressions on her face.

Rebecca Clites + ***Red Light, Green Light***

When my stepfather cut her head off
I ran, not the chicken.
She stood there silent—the quiet
blood dripping on her beautiful down.
I was not bleeding, but I was hurt.
The two of them stayed behind.
When I looked back, they waved,
as if to say, *Have a nice trip*.
Their lack of interest made me run faster
and further away from them.
I hurled a few bushes on the way
as I ran over the Pentagon.
The traffic light was so red I stopped
without taking a breath or drink.
My mind was on the axe.
Was it meant for me?
Did he mean to kill his stepdaughter?
Was it sharp enough to cut through
my thick skull with one blow?
Would he change his mind
half way through the deadly strike?
The brightness of the green told me
it was time to go.
I was parked and had to move.
When I returned home, only the
bloodstain remained on the table.

Deirdre Cooley + ***Imposter***

Breakfast in bed...
Self-prepared:
Eggbeaters, Velveeta, and Tang.

An Erector Set, without screws
Proposed on condition:
Of stringless secrecy and lies.

Substitutions and missing parts...
A counterfeit offering, bitterly enticing
To Miss LonelyHearts everywhere:

To awaken as a spoon,
Being slipped into...

Lusty musings intoxicate with fatal accuracy,
A creamy venom of paralyzing honey.

A plastic tale, specially concocted by the Imposter,
To satisfy his obsession
And slake his lust.

What is the cost of a spiritual patch?
Of saccharin salve,
Butter Buds, and broken things?

With a reluctant heart,
I weigh the potential damage
That Astroturf affection might exact.

The Monster of Lonely cares not,
Riled, reckless, and ravenous, is she.
Unslayable. Unslakeable. Unslaveable.

STOP! THINK!

The Imposter's lethal myth:
A bogus guarantee, rotting and putrid,
Promising a dearth of Empty.

How delicious, sex
If Cherish is absent?
How satisfying, orgasm
If Fondness and Laughter are missing?

This charlatan's epic is but a fabrication:
Now known to cause heartache and vomiting.
A sleep-induced revelation.

Void will return, uninvited.
Vengeful, disgusted, with fetters in hand...
And my emotional spackle will crumble.

Components of adoration, of love
Lost, astray... perhaps misplaced, like
Fresh-squeezed wing-nuts, buried in the backyard.

These circumstances are all wrong.
And he is not The One.

He is not the Object of my Desire,
This Imposter, my Tempter.
There is Another, Unwitting and Away.

Away, where Laughter and Intellect
Might revel, one day...
And lusty musings might be
As an Erector Set with all the screws,
As Eggs Benedict with jumbo yolks and hollandaise.

JD Cullum + *Twenty-Mop Poem*

They wadded up notes and slipped them into mop handles.
"I miss you, Baldy. Please kill me some Blacks.
"I miss you, Muttonchop. I killed you two blacks today."
"I'd write you a twenty-mop poem, if I had enough urine."
"Miss your sweet muttonchops between my legs.
"Now kill me a Wetback, if you please."
"I killed you a Wetback today, my love,
And I'm holding more office supplies up my ass."
"Sausage kisses for two. With toilet water."
The Charity Benefit Bikini Contest would go on as scheduled.
At this, two thousand fingers worked lotion onto four hundred hooters.
Celebrities shifted their cocks below cummerbunds.
And Masturbators saved their cum.
There will be no well-timed sneezes in the exercise yard!
Fingernail clippings are henceforth crucial.
And every mop handle, every wadded note,
And all that impersonates mop, handle, wad, note
Shall be vetted by people named Earl!
(Tourniquets garlanded the jailbirds' throats.
While the penguins admired the girls.)

I remember when I thought adults knew things. Before I became an adult myself and discovered how much everyone is just winging it.

The summer I was 13 years old, I asked my camp drama teacher, How do you know when you fall in love?

I didn't ask my mother that summer, who had met my father when she was 17, and 20 years later was still married to him. What did she know about falling in love? She married her high school sweetheart; she couldn't know about real life. Even their parents didn't trust their judgment: "Isn't it possible," my dad asked his mother when he was 17 and wore a leather bomber jacket, played high school football, and aspired to be the next JFK. "Isn't it possible," he replied to his mother, who cautioned him against exclusively dating my mother. "Isn't it possible," he demanded, "that you can pick the winning ticket on the first try?" How did that 17-year-old boy know about finding true love? How did that teenage kid trust his heart? How was he so wise?

I didn't trust my heart to know. I asked this young teacher, because she was cool, she was down, she was sexy, and—most significantly—she was not a mom and therefore might know a few things worth knowing.

I wanted a solid answer. I wanted, "You know you are in love and it is real because (a), (b), and (c)." I wanted the crib sheet, the answer page, the facts. I wanted reassurance that there are ways to know, that I *would* know when it happened. That I wouldn't miss it, or mistake something less for it.

We asked this drama coach, we 13-year-olds in her performing arts summer camp, we asked her during a break from practicing the songs and dances and words she had written for us to perform for our families and the friends they dragged there, friends who had known us since we were babies and who would leave during the intermission and break our hearts with their impatient coldness. We asked her to tell us what to look for in ourselves, what feelings we should recognize as the indicators of love. We wanted to know so we could have sex with someone we loved when we were 16, because we knew we weren't going to wait for marriage, but we wanted to at least wait for love.

We sat in a rough circle around her, brown bags crumpled with remains of our lunches—peanut butter and jelly sandwiches, apples, Fig Newtons, Hansen's sodas. We sat on the floor of the dance studio, smooth blond wood with specks of lint and dirt, scuffs from tap shoes and toe shoes and street shoes that should have been removed first but weren't. We sat there, reflected in the mirror, next to the piano we gathered around to learn the new songs, our backpacks and sweatpants and leg warmers tossed into one corner. It was the end of our day, and my 16-year-old older sister would be there in ten minutes to pick me up and drive us home, my sister who would not learn the answer we were anxious to hear for another 22 years, who would not learn it from the string of assholes she dated, who would not learn from her marriage and divorce, who would have her heart ripped up by hands, including her own, who would heal, crooked but still pumping every day, who would need a good answer soon, if not for herself, then for her own two daughters, and who by sheer-dumb-luck-miracle would meet her soul's match when she finally changed her mind and decided not to give up.

I wanted an answer.

And what did she say? Did she just say, "You'll know" and terrify us that we would have to look to ourselves, trust our own judgment, find and lose and find our own way? Did she say, "You'll know it's love when you find yourself with someone who allows you to be exactly who you are without even trying, who loves your mind and soul and body, in that order"?

Did she tell us that love will require us to take a leap of faith, that we may not know right away, that movies and rumors will lead us astray, looking for the sudden first feeling of delirium. Did she warn us how often that feeling would lead us to a sopping mess of How Could I Have Been So Stupid? Did she tell us that "falling in love" means that we have to jump and not look down, and that if we have found our Love, his tenderness will be our parachute? That love will ask us to let go of our fear and need for control, and ask us just to take a ride with an unknown conclusion?

Did she tell us to ask our parents?

All those sticky years ago, I remember. She did not promise that we would find love. She did not tell us what feelings we should feel. She did not give us an answer. She left it in our hands. She told us we would be all right, no matter what—whether or not we found what we thought we were looking for.

Julie Dolcemaschio + ***Hallelujah in C-minor***

—Per sempre, mio amore

How do I love thee?
I won't go there
I won't go where someone else has been
When you take a breath, I will take it away
When you take a step, I will trip you up
When you smile I will ache
To see it again

How do I love thee?
Please do not ask
I will show you without the words
You have heard before
When you call, I will echo your pain
When you cry, I will drown in your tears
Then wipe them away

How do I love thee?
I can't really say
Love is moments spent and
A lifetime lived
And the pain that comes from knowing
That you will never be loved
Like this again

How do I love thee?
So much you will ache to look at me
So much that you will cry for my touch
So much that I will destroy what keeps us apart
Even if it is for a little while
A little while is too long
Without your name, like honey, on my tongue

Denise Eldridge + ***An Ode to Wayward Bones***

I had wayward bones.
They lived beneath my skin—
Underneath the muscles, the tendons, the veins, the veinlets
Which pulsed and throbbed with the passage of my blood through
My body, over my wayward bones.

My wayward bones kept me at The Pelican night after night,
Countless evenings, a multitude of afternoons, a morning or two.
Tick tock—wristwatch.
Ding dong—grandfather clock.
A woman sang canticles in the corner.

My wayward bones and I sat languishing in the furthest nook of that
Cavernous pub, in the corners where no light would dare meander.
We sat among the questioners of life, the truth seekers, the very
Shallow and those whose depths caused such pain that they could
Only beg to escape the world beyond those walls;
The world beyond that crepuscular zone;
The world beyond arrival and departure.
And, only when my bones were ready, would they lead me home.

I think my bones are wayward still
Although the Pelican has closed down
Although I live in another country
Although they are far from the place where they were first formed.

I think my bones are less wayward and in different ways now that
They have no familiar place to slink into;
Now that the circle of my world has both contracted and expanded;
Now that time has passed and is passing still.

I think my bones are lazy now.
They are too content to keep up the endless search,
To keep the movement going,
To keep the pulse beating against the thin skin of my wrist.
The wanting and desire, the drive and need still exist in me but my
Bones are too content and I am afraid they have lost their wayward
Passion.
My bones are too content and I find myself, sometimes, crushed by
That contentment.
I mourn the loss of their waywardness;
I send laments up to the moon when she rises full in the sky.
I cry out,

Do you remember?
Do you remember?
Gnashing teeth and weeping for the absence I feel.
For those wayward bones, in their longing for understanding,
In their desire to be unfettered,
In their need to find safe harbor,
Those bones are the best of me.

I like the smell of dog, the wetter the better; a musky earthy smell. And I like the sound of dog too, the snoring and dreaming sounds of aborted barks and whimpers trying to escape the paralysis of sleep. Sometimes the paws do escape and the beagle paddles the air thinking she's going somewhere. But not Sophie. She is old and big and has learned an economy of movement so I have to look closely to see the twitches and quivers of a lip, a paw, an eyelid.

She's a trusty hound in brown and black and a muzzle gone grey. The vet says she's at death's door, but I'm thinking she got the diagnosis wrong, cause Sophie ain't buying it and appears to have decided to live forever. Just the same, we've let down the rules around here because a dog in her last months deserves a nice couch to sleep on and lots of milkbones. I have a special place in my heart for milkbones.

When I was six my dad said, "Close your eyes and I'll give you a surprise." So I did, and I waited, smiling, anticipating, imagining what always came next, a chocolate caramel coconut Yum Yum cookie, my favorite. Dad kept a stash of them, in that bachelor's apartment whose cupboards had only two things: a case of tuna fish and yum yums. That's how he'd lived after my mother dumped him for Seymour, the swashbuckling bon vivant who helped her forget she was his wife and, oh yeah, our mother. Dad never recovered and his cupboards stayed bare, except for tuna and yum yums.

I kept my eyes closed hard, against the yellow light spilling into that apartment kitchen, light that ignored the curtains some aunt had donated in an effort to add a 'woman's touch' to the place. She failed. Sounds of dump truck burped up from the alley below. I'd braced myself against the counter of that galley kitchen and waited for the ritual wafer from my holy father. And it came. And I knew it was good, before I ever bit down. And then I bit down. But holy wasn't exactly on the menu that day, or maybe it was just replaced by mischief, because what I tasted was not coconut or anything else I knew. It wasn't sweet or chewy or familiar, but dry and dusty and tasteless. That's when I learned what milkbone tasted like, that's when I stopped understanding why dogs eat them. So now, every time I give Sophie a milkbone, which she thinks is just grand, I can't help feeling guilty that these things really suck and if she only knew, she wouldn't think I was so great.

Perspective. It's everything. I woke up at 4 A.M. yesterday morning. Disturbed. These days I wake up and gauge the feeling: anxiety, anticipation, joy. And then I work backwards to become conscious of why I would be feeling that and remember what's bothering me, what I'm looking forward to, what the day holds for me. Yesterday it was doom. The thought went something like this: I'm still me; shit. But I am. I am wondering where's those fat little Disney fairies that came to Sleeping Beauty when her lights went out? I want my epiphany. I want to wake up and have a reason. That was not yesterday. "Get out, walk" those fat fairies would have yelled. So I did. To the beach, my personal cure for everything that ails me. Four miles, one journal and a cappuccino later and things usually right themselves. Only it didn't work. And it didn't help that a movie crew had infested my space, which was now overrun with preteens and body piercings, and a crew of hip underpaid 20-somethings who would have made more money at McDonalds or at least enjoyed health benefits, but traded that for the oh-so-cool of scrounging crumbs in "the industry." I parked the car and got out. And was hit by a wall of cigarette smoke that had settled like a cloud over their territory at only eight in the morning. My beach had become their territory. They'd barricaded my path with reflector umbrellas and cables and mountains of equipment and bodies loitering and I wanted to yell, clean up your room. But instead, I mustered; the strength, the determination to plow thru their mess like an invisible bowling ball. There was an eerie quiet, as if something important was happening. I think it was actually boredom punctuated by slight adjustments to their ipods which kept them insulated in their own little worlds while they waited. That's what crews do, they wait. But it wasn't my thing, so I plowed because the only way is thru and I am learning to go through.

Michelle Fiordaliso + ***The Underworld***

I choose calla lilies for my credenza, white or green ones. They seem to fit with the room, clean and art deco. Today, I bought peonies instead. Pink ones that don't really match with the red vase or the rest of the decor. They cost more than the calla lilies but I wanted them. There's a photo of me at three years old in my backyard next to a pink peony bush. There are balls of pink behind me, none of them in bloom. A peony plant healed Hades, God of the underworld. I recently heard a retelling of the myth of Persephone and Hades. In this one, she isn't forced to the underworld like the rape myth that we've all heard before. No, in this one, she sees Hades and is enchanted by him. I mean she really likes the guy despite his darkness, you know what I'm saying. She willingly goes to him. She tastes the pomegranate as she's leaving and so she's forced to return every year for six months. Makes you think maybe she knew exactly what she was doing, maybe she invited the option of returning. Either way, her world, was forever changed, like so many other times in history, by a mouthful of sweet fruit.

Michael, my son's father, pulled a cold mango out of the fridge after we had sex. He sliced the ripe fruit against his finger. The juicy yellow rested on the blade. The steel edge of the blade was so close to my tongue. It was summer in New York, and we made love to the sounds of the remote controlled air conditioner. The heat and the city making our skin moist and dirty but it didn't matter. It wasn't the first time he'd fed me fruit after fucking. It was something he did and I liked it. Michael told me that when he was a boy in Iran, his father used to separate the seeds of the pomegranate for him and put them in bowls where he wouldn't have to work so hard for the few glistening bits of juice. He hasn't seen his father in thirty years. He doesn't want to. In that summer, Michael and I met, made a baby and then, by the following summer he was gone. He gives our son fruit now, sends him home with Ziploc bags of pomegranate seeds or berries. Michael let the mango drop onto my tongue—the blade never came close enough to hurt me. He knew exactly when to pull it away

There's a retelling of my story too. I willingly let my son's father love me the way his father taught him to love. He loved me by feeding me fruit, by filling me with a child and then, by leaving. Yes, that's right, he left me by leaving. The peonies on my credenza opened today—spread themselves apart revealing their featherlike fragrant insides—so huge despite their delicate red stems. I wonder if they can heal me like they healed Hades. In the photo of me at three the peonies are frozen in closed blossoms. I suppose they bloomed someday. I'd like to believe they did.

Julia Soto Frazer + ***Four Poems for the Tale of Genji by Murasaki Shikibu***

The Rowboat

My legs, like reeds, planted in brackish water,
my arms, floating at my sides,
I look to sea.

Mud rolls off my body and I am clean.
I row. My sleeves move in triangular dips.

No companion.

The Bed

This book so heavy, black ink falling
between sheets. I search for words,
my sleeves smeared with blood.

It will soon be over.

June nightingale.

The Bird

Cave heart awake with birdsong.
I listen, stilled by joy.

Reaching for the curtain, my sleeves fall open.

It was I all along.

The Woman

The fragrance follows. No matter. I
know no other perfume. I walk,
trailing sweetness.

Happy the one who sees all
and hopes for nothing.

Ashes where I sit.

I had my hand on the brown burl marble counter when the concierge desk attendant said "diarrhea," there in the sparkle-clean morning tonic of ammonia and glass cleaner. The word seemed more vulgar than usual, and then perfectly Colombian as well.

I looked down onto the pool, the extra large square that had a dark blue bottom, with striped cushions on white plastic lounge chairs which sunk into the shallow end. They got 'em positioned so you could drop a toe or an arm into the cold when the sun got too much. I hate David Hockney, but I felt like I was in his world, like I was living in the beautiful and clean eighties, like I was rich in Palm Springs. A porter scrubbed the pool's edge with Ajax, blue clairvoyant pitch, peddling gaminas selling Chiclets. I'm a million miles from the Mars Bar on second, where you could lose a month just drinking beer. I'm 34 now, too old for the 17-year-old model I met last night; I'm too old to make my hands seem worthwhile to her, too old to put my mouth where she sits. I'm desperate for one last moment of really hot.

"Oh, god" I squeal to myself like a fag, make that brown marble burl a virus that glorifies every inch of me like a David Katz complexion. Give me a pool drink and a million dollars. "I don't care," I say. "I love them."

I'm eating my third granillia; I'm addicted to the orange pear-shaped fruit with its hard shell. Two in each hand, I'm cracking them hand over fist like a body builder stacking yokes. Inside is a white cotton sack, pregnant with these little jelly-covered seeds that dangle on wormed glow plugs. I have a fluffy pod propped up between my top and bottom front teeth, and my tongue is diligently digging into the seeds, gently separating them from their seats, like a lassoed loose tooth being slammed out of a baby's mouth with a door.

When the man says "diarrhea," my hand fists against the brown burl marble for traction. I bite down on the jelly hard stuff and stare at his starched black jacket and tie. He's a fat cadaver dipped in jelly bobbing to the tune of Vivaldi. I am sticky from defrocked granillia that I knew was not her, and it was never gonna be her again. August is over, the Mars Bar closed for transfusions, everything is new in that chlorine kinda way, and I am watching the last skid of really hot slide by.

Tim Giblin + ***Mexico's last***

I'm heading backwards on the road from Comitan to Armatrillo, backwards into the long pine forests of Chiapas, backwards away from the border of Mexico, away from the armed guards, away from the fat border officials, back towards the Israeli woman. Backwards. The fields by the side of the road are on fire, and the hot blaze and smoke reach out to the leaking fumes of my gas tank, another casualty of the roads another warning on the uphills and downhills, on the broken gravel, to all those that pass, that animals and children live here. beware, slow down, obey, those are the signs on the back roads of Chiapas, those are the signs that I am following as I head backwards. I look out onto matchbook squares of dirt. Black and white bulls, with horns and a swollen hump, sows with long necklace ears of lapis, over sweet black noses, black rocks, porous from thirsty flames stacked like pearls on a debutantes neck, stacked and plowed by a wooden rake two inches deep in a trough of Zapatista tears. Torn and mended, purple and white scarves like anenomies in a tide blow up women's backs carrying babies and oranges to Amatrillo, backwards to me.

I was gonna enter Guatemala today but I forgot my camera in a small hotel in Amatrillo, a two-street dirt town off the main road between Palenque and San Christobal. I dropped off the Israeli girl in the bus station in Palenque, told her to go to the Yucatan. I told her about the Caribbean Sea, and the coves of Tulum. I kneeled over her in Palenque and emptied my meanness onto her chest, turned away from her demands, and left her alone. I don't want anyone to see me cross the border, see me lose faith, lose dignity, lose control. Another border, another heartbreak, another new kind of alone, and the fires are hot and the smoke threatens and I swerve to avoid a bloated white burrow who has been hit by a truck, bloodied bowels oozing backwards from its furry rectum; its brother or sister dares me with pitiful eyes under long lashes and a leather bridle torn at the reigns. *Stay back,* I whisper, half to me, half to the burrow, and a fantasy half to the Israeli, as she cleans her chest with a white towel from the bathroom, curling up into a ball at my feet. The bed is cramped and I hear the oscillating fan skip a turn, banging, banging against plastic blades, and a bent cage, banging against Palenque, banging against borders and women, and me, banging into the morning, broken and alone.

Kathleen Zeisler Goldman + ***mary wants to remember***

cleaning day
dust all gone
dishes stacked
everything in its place
i don't see the crucifix
this goes here
that goes there
i can't remember things
there goes here
that goes this
nothing is where I left it
my mother
agnes
is dead
that other
says she's my sister
and a girl
calls me mom
some days they
look like agnes who
does what
goes where
cook cook cook
cook the dinner
the potatoes are
what's the word
missing
and the dishes
who goes
what
this goes that
I hid money
hid me too
where goes mary
this what
this rosary
this wedding ring
this eternal soul

Teri Goldman + ***Flirtations***

I am starting to talk to fruit. Seriously, I walked away from a young, hunky, luscious, drag-me-down-to-the-ground New Zealander at my co-op today, a man who I was sure had no interest in me because I was fresh-out-of-yoga-class-grungy, attired in sweats and no make-up. Only after I had taken my veggie juice from the counterperson and said a casual goodbye did I second-guess the situation, but it was too late. Instead of turning back to get his number, I came home and spoke to the fruit bowl. Now, it's not unusual for me to walk away from men out of shyness, or for me to speak to the fruit flies, scolding them for hovering all around my apartment. But, today, I lifted the little white mesh cover that detours the less-intelligent flies and asked the fruit which pieces were ripe enough to go into the fridge. A couple white peaches and nectarines volunteered a moldy spot or a soft, spongy feel. As I removed the blemishes, I realized that talking to fruit could be a sign that I am spending too much time by myself, that the fine line between "rejuvenating downtime" and "introverted, hermit-like behavior" may be blurring in my abode. Let's face it: the fruit doesn't really want to be bothered.

I feel fairly secure in my fruit conversing skills. Men are another story. Flirtatious is my middle—or perhaps my fourth or fifth—name when I am drawn out, but self-induced eye batting is challenging for me. My friend Roxanne attracts men like fruit flies; while I...well...I just attract the flies. Roxanne has a natural, sexy, East Coast confidence in her swagger, a "kiss me and you will be in for the ride of your life" kind of aura. I have a "quiet intellectual in glasses" kind of aura, even though I don't wear glasses. I am the woman one meets perusing a bookstore or touring a Van Gogh exhibit midday. Dressed in jeans and a tee shirt, I meander through the museum gallery, pausing to read each and every word of each and every description beside each and every photo or painting or sculpture. I possess that kind of intense, curious, absorbed-in-something-bigger-than-myself air that was sexy to men when I was ten years younger. Now, I think it reads more old, staid, don't mess with me, boring librarian than anything else—at least in this town, where young, hot, and glitzy is what counts.

The irony is that I'm rather warped and kooky around people who know me, and I have inherited my parents' biting sense of humor. My family teased me about my inability to take a joke when I was younger, but I grew to understand the absurdity of their logic. I mean, who in their right mind uses sarcasm on a three-year-old and expects the child to not take it personally? Therapy, therapy, therapy, therapy, life is but a dream analysis. It makes me laugh...now. Laughter, how I love laughter. Yet, lately, full belly chuckles elude me. I think about meeting someone with whom to build a peaceful, fulfilling, deep, spiritual and silly life, and the daunting nature of the task pummels me. I want all the great parts of a relationship and all the difficult facets and so much more laughter; but the process of going to events, putting profiles on the Internet, volunteering, speed dating, and all the other bizarre things that a sexy librarian impersonator needs to do to meet the right guy seems overwhelming. Sometimes I think it's this town, where everyone wants and expects perfection from everyone else.

I miss New York. In the city, I can walk down the street in a torn t-shirt, all 38 years of me with no makeup, sweating like a pig and smelling of subway stench, and I still get hit on. New Yorkers like the hot librarian schoolmarm fantasy. Roxanne also emerges from the fog around East Coast men. She's the bad news that could eat them for lunch, and one never gains weight in New York no matter what one consumes. The speed, the tenacity, and the drive of the city all make meeting people or not meeting people so much easier. I'm not saying that relationships turn out any better, or that East Coast men are not cads sometimes. They are just more direct about it. For this indirect woman with a heart of gold upon a fortress of rocks and chasms, that directness is just fucking hot—like the summer, and the humidity, the sweat dripping from my cleavage, slipping down into my groin. And, I'm here in Los Angeles, and the August heat is so very cold. Roxanne says that she is going to drag my ass out soon. I tell her she had better, because it's getting awfully big sitting at home on the sofa with a piece of fruit, a book in hand, and computer glasses for the librarian schoolmarm effect.

Helen Halverson + ***Escape***

My German Shepherd is named Rambi because he looks like Rambo and usually acts like Bambi. He mourned with me when Sam died. He nestled in Sam's old shirt on the floor on Sam's side of the bed while I slept off the drugs that got me away from all the people downstairs.

When I woke up in the dark, I was already standing in the doorway.

Rambi was downstairs barking and growling in the kitchen. He didn't stop, didn't seem to breathe, sounding like the crazed, slobbering attack dogs shown in a documentary which were trained by Hitler's storm troopers to kill prisoners who had tried to escape.

Escape. I have to escape. Or hide. Burglar. Thief.

Snarls, lower growls. Rambi doesn't stop.

I can't help him. Can't move. Must move. Must hide. Run. Run where? Out the window. Second storey, can't jump.

Rambi doesn't stop—snarling, barking, growling, still in kitchen at back door.

Go to window. Won't open. Lock is stuck. Run to closet. Light automatically comes on in closet. Scent of leather shoes. Too many black clothes. Half of closet is empty. Light glares off empty hangers. Hide the light. Close door. No light, dark in closet. Find shoe. Creep to door. Quick open door. Light comes on. Damn. Crash through door and slam shut on light. Too much noise. Must hide in dark.

Rambi only snarling and growling now. No barking.

Use shoe to hit window lock. Again. Too much noise. Burglar will hear me. Hit one more time. Lock turns. Open window. Too far down. Can't see. Why is front porch light off? We . . . I . . . have a chain fire-escape ladder. Where is chain ladder? Under bed? No. Don't look in closet; too empty, too much light. Did Sam put rolled up chains near window? Can't remember.

Rambi still snarling, growling. Barking too. Kitchen door.

Sam told me. What did he say? Can't think; can't hear his voice. Can't see. Tears again. And again.

So much Rambi noise. Echoes. Hits my ears. Can't breathe. Rambi doesn't stop. Doesn't breathe.

Can't breathe.

Sam rolled up escape ladder. Damn Sam for dying. Can't find ladder. Crawling around on floor. Chains should be near window. Hit forehead on dresser. Pain. Can't think.

Rambi still gets louder, more ferocious. Like a killer.

A killer coming into my house. Forget chain ladder. I'll just jump. And run.

Rambi whimpers. No noise.

Killer will come up stairs. Crawl to doorway. Close door on killer. Chain ladder behind door.

No noise.

Too heavy. Must carry. Can't carry. Grab hook part. Drag. Chains bang. Too much noise. Killer will know I'm up here. Can't run. Too much noise. Chains drag on floor, catch on rug. Yank. And pull. Fall to one knee on top of chain. Pain.

Dizzy. Need oxygen. Breathe through mouth. Taste blood.

Rip rug.

No noise down stairs. Poor Rambi.

Tears. Nose running. Wipe on pajamas. Hurry. Hurry. Must get out. Drag ladder to window.

Dark. Can't see. Blood running into right eye. Wipe on pajama sleeve, already wet.

Chain's hook is backwards. Crying. Sobbing. Too much noise. Killer will hear. Chains too heavy.

Light. Coming under hallway door. Killer is here. Throw chains out now. Hurry. Now. Arms shaking. Now. Only one hook works. Damn.

Rambi barks again. One bark. Maybe he's okay.

I'm not okay. Must get out. Must get out. Must get out. Escape. Chains clatter down side of house. Other hook is bent. Won't work. One will have to do. Hurry. Hurry. Now.

Put foot out of window. Can't find step. Cold. Scrape on bare foot. Pain. Back down. Another step. Hit back of neck against window frame. More pain. Falling.

Alice Hayward + ***L.A. Vertigo***

Vicious water lilies disguised as lotus
slash through the muck of Echo Park Lake.
Machete leaves gouge their silhouettes into the L.A. skyline.
The Bonaventure Hotel bites its thumb at you sir.
Traffic stitches its way up and down the streets,
up and down the lurid neon synapses of my brain.
This is the city, the big city,
where anything can happen to an ingénue in chaps.
Yippee-ky-yea-ky-yea!
It's not only dominatrixes
that get hog tied and branded in L.A.

The inverted red heart of her ass wobbles down the street,
her compact mirror shows two vermilion lips
lost through lack of reflection.
Rumplestiltskin is not her name,
and she has no tresses to lower to waiting lovers,
only sagging breasts as she hovers above them.
Her vaginal lips applaud her lost dreams.
Moccasins and marshmallows and seamed stockings
are the apex of Native American contemporary twisted glamour.
Crotchless fluorescent polish on grim nails
are a hooker's beasty fiend.
Esther Williams parts the waters of his mustache
slick with Vitalis.
Cheap patent leather shoes pinch in the heat
and—look
So—cool!

Trailer parks glitter with Christmas lights in July,
aluminum subterfuge to cover damaged souls.
The Salvation Army is reprimanded for tax evasion.
Insomnia soders me to the Jerry Springer show
where groveling is the forte.
Puking and fucking become elevated,
as Agamemnon tweaks her nipple,
Pliny pleads with Hippocrates for enough Nyquil
to make this all worthwhile.
The woolly mammoths beneath La Brea sleep in prehistoric bliss.
Dreams of vertigo do not disturb their petrified alpha waves.
Monuments of solemn taxidermy. Trigger pleads to Roy and Dale for a sarcophagus,
or a makeover and a tail lift.

Don't—I
At—least
Deserve—that?
But the Compton drive-through mortuary is not having a special,
so tough patutti.

Gene Autry's wives could have done you better in Griffith Park.
Forest Lawn is so passé'.
I do embrace cryonics
so my beers will truly be the coldest in town.
Figueroa threads its way through black and white and yellow.
The best kosher burritos are sold in Chinatown.
The Westside restlessly lolls and waits to be rediscovered
by he who is firm and well hung in bank account and dick.
Venice is drying out for the seventieth time
and rehabilitating the hairless Hari Krishnas,
Baldheads gleam like honey drops in the sunset,
as they invade Marina del Rey's Silver Strand
where Pillsbury doughboy computer geeks populate the high-rises
destroying the wetlands with their webbed foot web sites.

What Boeing flights of fancy
wear Fredrick's of Hollywood garter belts with support hose?
The residential facilities of my mind
regurgitate dreams verathaned with half digested cotton candy.
My—life
has—been
farted—away
single handedly causing the greenhouse effect.
If gas prices are no longer soaring,
why is my savings account starving?
This famine has reach my soul
and crowned it with a 99-Cent Store tiara.
Rhett Butler arises from between my legs
And Frankie still don't give a damn.

Starbucks rape virgin territory adjacent to national parks,
Sabado Gigante makes "lame" an understatement,
Third world countries want to grow lust—like—us.
Miss Cleo lays the Tarot cards to predict that
Mr. Blackwell will put the Statue of Liberty on his worst dressed list.
The hope for the future is based
on someone,
anyone,
joining the Knights of the Garter,
with a seersucker Ph.D. in nuclear physics,

by the end of this month.
Out!
Out, dammed spot!
New and improved laundry products can save us all.

I read the Stinky Cheese Man in pornographic bliss.
My drool cup runneth over
as George W. Bush unleashes Mexican truck drivers
to cross international borders to remove lint from my navel.
My hula-hoop vibrates in anticipation.
What
a—time
I—live—in.
Casting directors wring their hands,
Macarthur Park rubber bands cocaine and cunt together
while shitting Otis Parsons to extinction.
Interactive singles saunter down La Cienega
and those on Santa Monica
politely fence their way into algebraic brassieres

L.A.'s sin
Is indifference.

My crime
Is my birth.

Vertigo,
Vertigo,
Vertigo.

Mary Holmes + *The Nature of Travel*

The rainfall
forms a river
that tumbles over rocks
down the mountain
becoming a waterfall
immersing me
allowing me
to witness my own baptism,

I am every drop of water.

Carved out of a cliff
overlooking the valley
the spirit of ecstasy
leans into the wind
names every leaf and shadow
listens to ancestral ghosts
traces every wild horse and wish
released and long ago forgotten,

I am standing in the shadow.

A woman sits
in a room made of amber
filled with honey colored light
in search of the origin of wonder
while whole schools of fish
make the silvery choice
to change direction
without hesitation or debate,

I am that woman.

A dragonfly circles
palaces, museums
and orchards of glory
before coming to rest
on an avalanche,

I go along for the ride.

Sipping jasmine tea
deep inside the rainforest

I wait

I watch

as dust settles
on the history of history.

Mary Holmes + *When I Go*

Shaking newborn limbs
investigate the atmosphere
fragile, unfettered
I will take that with me
when I go.

Tracking the passing of a leaf,
or the movement of an insect,
or the lament of one note
leaning hard against departure,
I feel a smooth steel ball
spinning in my chest.
I barely see an injured blue bird,
a ball gown that won't dance
but keeps turning
over and over anyway.
An invitation not answered,
a phone call not returned,
a life half lived.

I will take that with me when I go.

"Don't look at me like that,"
comes straight out of nowhere,
and suddenly the world goes naked,
down to the last molecule.
Which one said it first
doesn't really matter.

The deviant surprise—
I'm looking for it.
Throwing up frames
at odd angles,
against the glass,
against the gray,

against that particular afternoon,
searching for memories
waiting to happen.
I will take that
with me when I go.

Baby thunder
is setting off the primitives
while a stick of sunlight
pierces a cloud,
the ground, my iris.
Hesitation indicating
not so much melancholy
or even nostalgia
but that slight nod,
almost invisible now
built in, that acknowledges
the protocols of the heart,
a tiny reward, straight up.

These moments,
pressed like a work shirt
with that hot clean cotton smell,
or the glimmering edge of a diamond
reflecting light bouncing in
from an unknown source,
or something as easily worn
as a favorite pair of shoes,
are no less dear,
no less vivid,
still not strangers.

I will take them,
all of them, with me
when I go.

Laurie Brooks Jefferson + ***Oakland to L.A.***

Doing fifty
on the 580.
Past Home Depot,
Sav-On,
Target, a red bull's eye,
past hills full of windmills,
like the pinwheels I blew on
as a child.
I made them spin
black and silver
into the wind.

Doing 60
on the 580 takes me
to the I-5,
away from my daughter
and her husband,
away from the tract house
and laughter
from their bedroom
in the mornings.
Lover's giggles
and long silences.
The arms and legs in that room
must tie themselves into bows,
lips kissing eyes and noses
and that tender flesh
below the ear.

At 70 miles an hour
I pass herds of cows
eating grass in pastures
one blade at a time.
I pass a dark man
who has stopped
to check his boat.
I will never know him.
We will never go fishing
or fuck in the back
of his pickup,
or even share a beer
on its hood

under the big dipper
on the fourth of July
as fireworks splash
the coast with sparks.
I'm rolling now
past rows of almond trees
in straight lines
along dry river beds,
their rocks exposed
like genitals,
and there
the seeded dirt ferments
under high tension lines.
And I want to follow any exit
that could send me
back into the wind
toward my daughter,
but the image of my car
is flattened out
behind a gasoline truck
whose steel hind-end
has turned my reflection
into a compressed vision
of jailed motion.

So I push to 80 instead,
past thousands of cows
standing in their excrement,
waiting to be slaughtered,
past the Chevron truck
in order to feel round again,
past the broken white line
in the middle of the road,
past the sign with yellow letters
warning travelers of high winds,
winds revved by pinwheels,
the breath of children
blowing me into the future,
spinning me silver,
spinning me black,
spinning me toward death.

Kurt Kamm + ***Sarah's Song of the Investigation of Immobilization***

We are vesicles encapsulated
in the
interlocked consequences of our phases

Forsake the
rationale of the ultra-incompressible

Gain considerable attention and
generate action through self assembly

We must change orientation
and find fast events
flowing on the pathway to higher replication

Ascend to the ultimate understanding of
the exchange between two repeats

Shadow great insight in
exposed disengagement

Overcome the diversity generating pattern
of blinding hardness

Execute restricted steps
Visualize the nontrivial link

The examples of salutary imperative
are demonstrated by foul events

Mimic
Synthesize
Consume
Enable

SARAH, I STAND CONFLECTED

Jean Katz + ***Laotian Children***

At the sandy shore of the Mekong River
the boatman lays a narrow board for a gangplank.
Strangers' hands reach out to guide me across.
I look up to see a skinny Asian cow and calf,
the same color as the sand where they
graze on the meager grass shoots.

Then I look higher to see young children
scamper up and down very tall trees,
fabric bags slung across their shoulders
and long knives in their hands.
"What in the world are they doing?" I ask.
"Harvesting teak seeds," the guide replies.
"Only the young children can climb that high
and have the branches support them."
It reminds me of Papua, New Guinea
where I once saw young children
harvest cocoanuts from palm trees
with scythes as big as they were.

After we climb a steep, sandy embankment,
the village teacher shows us his one-room schoolhouse.
Young children run past us in packs.
It is a holiday, so no one is in school.
Some play cards in the dirt beside the school.
A young teenage girl walks by,
two pails balanced on a pole across her shoulder,
carrying stones to build a second room on the school.

Every house is on stilts, to stay dry
when the water of the Mekong rises.
Women sit in the shade under their houses,
weaving the silk stoles they press us to buy.
Their infants ride around town
on the hips of eight-year-old brothers and sisters.

I picture my three grandchildren here,
running free as Laotian children,
and taking on jobs no one expects of them at home,
where they fight for free time
between car pools, lessons, and play-dates.

Judi Kaufman + *Eye Pillow*

I am taking the time to remove my eye pillow
A tool to help me see when I am blind sighted.
The eternal pillow mom gave me.
Leave my vision alone, my eyes are burning.
Stay out of my way from my evergreen limbs.
I have become an openhearted woman,
Despite the spite and split in my body.
I stand on my head while managing my heart and my heat.
It is my eye pillow of satin and lavender.
I'm a worm watching exquisite flowers stand still in their splendor.
Along my journeys I have seen Egyptian pyramids.
The war is in the Middle East.
I am in the middle of a personal war, my personal map.
Don't steal my eye pillows, I remove it with breath.
My dreams; my light—all a lonely journey.

Marley K.D. + ***Into the Fire***

—or Why I'm Not Tipper Gore

So here was my thinking: when he was a little more than a year old I'd strap him to me, jump in the subway and go to a piano brunch. He'd stand still on a chair, my arm around his soft solid body, watching the fingers on the keyboard as long as the man was playing.

When he was two and a half, I took him to see Barney at Radio City Music Hall. After burying his head in my shoulder in terror at seeing so many people in one room, he sat still on my lap, his fingers wrapped tight around one of my thumbs, watching, unaware of the mother-sitter-toddler chaos all round us.

At eight, he leaned in close, fitting fully under my arm in cold seats on a far edge of the Hollywood Bowl to hear Weird Al Yankovic.

Now he's turning thirteen, a dark, angry, no-touching thirteen. When I reach for him he bends away like a cat: he's close, can feel the heat of the human, but the whisper of air, the momentum of away, feels like gone. His music is so loud now, the basic self-care so poor, I blow right by the eyeliner and heavy black boots worn in summer to argue pathetically about hearing and dental loss, homework not done or worse: done, crumpled up, and not turned in. I tell myself this is just another wave, no different than ripples of obsessions that have come and gone, rolling breakers of Raffi and Pokemon and Star Wars and Bionicles and war games. But, is it?

He's on line, typing, long hair over his face. The sound of someone coming in doesn't make him look up. He's not interested. "Luke, you want to go to Ozzfest?"

"With you?" I can see one blue eye.

"Well, you're not going without me."

He's thinking. The trade-off isn't going my way.

"You can pretend I'm not there. So long as you agree not to go into the pit or out of my sight except to go to the bathroom or get food, no one will be able to tell you're with me."

"Yeah?"

"Yeah."

"Okay."

Well, it seemed like a good idea. Barney, Weird Al, Ozzy Osborne—what's the difference? But then I learned that it's fourteen hours long. But then I learned that it's outside, in the end of July, in the part of California that spontaneously combusts in summer. But then I learned that there were no seats for us, no shade of any kind anywhere in the amphitheater, and no backpacks or blankets or chairs allowed through the gate.

I soon found out why.

A highway through flat, dead, hills comes to a rude end at an amphitheater whose name keeps changing when one low-rent corporation or another stops paying. Every car in line is larger and louder, cleaner and darker than our dusty silver van. Luke had spent days on line checking out the bands, telling me each change, talking to me every night in the weeks leading up to the day. The full, little-boy eye contact was almost overwhelming sweet, overwhelming sad. I sat in it, felt it, aware of all the times I hadn't noticed, hadn't fully felt it, grabbed it, known it was precious and wouldn't last forever. It isn't until we're on our way in the car that I realize I hadn't actually heard a lot of what he's been telling me for weeks. He's saying names of bands, names like: blood dripping down, needles in my eyes, every time I die, death, death, gory bloody death. And I've been saying, "That's nice, sweetheart. Oh, really? That's great."

Well, fourteen hours from now I'll be back in this van driving away from these dry scrubby treeless hills. Fourteen hours from now.

Fourteen hours.

We park seemingly at random on an unmarked open dirt field pockmarked by grass and join the flow of sour ghouls, all hair gel and steel, heading for the gate. Once through the metal detectors that rejected no one but those carrying backpacks of water, we passed by the cinderblock concession stand, a white tin truck selling beer and another selling black festival shirts for 35 dollars apiece, all already overwhelmed with people. Luke tries to walk ahead, but there are never more than two strangers between us. When I stop to buy water, I don't have to motion or call him. He stops, two strangers away.

There are a few other parents of underage kids here and there in the crowd. We recognize each other by our uniform: we're the only people not wearing black, we're all carrying plastic bottles of sunscreen and big, thick, serious-looking books.

Hour after hour, longhaired muscled clones howl, scream and swear in sun so hot and dry it feels life threatening. I had warned of mosh pits but knew nothing about the body-slamming vortexes that suddenly spring mid-crowd; the sweating, stamping, trampling, whirling crowd throws up a hurricane of brown dust so thick it's actually blots out part of the stage, part of the heavy, metal poles holding the red and black band banners that only differ in their choice of death icons.

Unhappy that we're so far away, Luke's lying on his side on the slight hill, his rounded, I-don't-care back towards me. I'm now sitting on the book I brought in and I've given up trying to hear differences between bands and started counting the number of spoken f@#ks. Sung f@#ks are too hard to decipher; that would require being able to discern separate and discreet words in the amplified and distorted howls. The average spoken f@#ks in a 15-minute set is seventeen. Well, until Super Joint Ritual came on. A bell-curve-violating one hundred and three. One hundred and three spoken f@#ks in a thirty-minute set. A virtuoso performance using the word as a noun, verb, adverb, expletive, adjective and, my personal favorite, as a term of endearment. As in "a f@#king amazing f@#ker that guy."

F@#k.

By the time the sun was flat in our faces, I thought the worst was over. Yes, the acrid smell of bad dope and spilled beer was thicker, but bands with names I recognized began and the severe, sharp faces meant to shock started becoming a dusk-joined anonymous crowd. Everything seemed to soften, slow…at least at first. But dehydration and hours of legal and illegal substances are a rough mix.

Luke's voice is right beside me. "Slayer's next. Can we go closer?"

Closer means standing. Closer means risk. Closer is closer. Closer is just us.

"Okay."

Sixty thousand people are here tonight, most of them on what's called the lawn, most of them jammed along the edge closest to the stage. Moving forward we have to slalom through the tiniest gaps between bodies, small groups of drunk boys, leather coats lying open under couples on the ground, lone long haired men looking too hard for places to belong, crushed cups that skitter and crunch. The long slow fade from blues to black is now through and the only light comes from the scaffolded towers on either side of us along with the blinking, brief lightening bug flares of lighters and matches in the crowd around us. The smell of dirt and smoke and dirty clothes worn too long makes the crowd intimate, knowing, one.

In the dark Luke and I look so different from what we are. He forgets he's taller, broader. So do I. I lead to break through. I lead to take care. He looks hard after me in the dark, following each step, feeling safe, protected by the tiny woman he looks down on.

To our right, a bare-chested, balding, sunburned guy starts slamming into one person after another and we see, first hand, the birth of a vortex. We start to back away but suddenly there's a glow, a new charged knot in the crowd, behind us.

A fire.

They've set the trash on fire.

And then another.

A vortex to the left, and two fires behind us.

A frightened line of yellow-shirted security boys toting a water tank is trotting towards the largest, while shapes that belong on cave walls start flying around the other. Moving the only direction possible, we stop at the first place where we can see the stage, an informal aisle between us and a large sloppy group on the ground. There's room here, room to see, room to run if we have to.

I'm in charge of escape routes but, beside me, arm pressed against my arm, Luke's knowing all the words, the unbelievably hideous words, shouting them in chorus with all the throats all around him when a drunk couple crashes into us. The white, dredlocked woman's muscular bare arms reach out from inside a loose black vest and her thick, khaki-covered legs are wrapped tightly around the skinny, dirty guy who's having a hard time carrying her anywhere. A small set of bulbous wooden beads on three strands of rough leather dangle off the side of her neck. There is a pause, a lost in time where we are a foursome, a unit, a group, a family, alone, in silence, together, apart. In the glow of the fires I can see her face, lines spraying out from the corners of her eyes. From age or from drugs, how old is she? I can't tell but then how is it that I am so certain that we know them as well as they know each other, that whatever is happening is brief, now, and soon to be over. I don't know how I know, but I do.

They look at me. They look at Luke. They look back at me and the decision is made.

They fall to the ground, the toes of one of my feet underneath the clump of bodies, and they start to mate. A grasping, groping, rutting in the dirt.

Luke tries not to look.

As if a new, unexpected thought just occurred to me, I look up at my son: "I think we should move over there."

"Good idea."

He leads. I follow.

On stage, it's now raining blood. Standing in the new pocket we've found between the hurricanes of people to the left and right and the fires behind us, I see the jaw, the nose, the brow of a man in the dark red light from the stage and know it won't be long before he'll realize I have no right to stand between him and the crowd.

And I am no longer afraid.

With a voice hoarse from joyous screaming, Luke brushes his hair out of his face as he leans in close to shout: "Thanks, Mom."

Catherine Klatzker + ***Comfort Food***

A comforting yeasty smell pushes against
My nostrils, draws me into her kitchen
Raw mix of flour strains against

The dishtowel on the oversized bowl
Two strong musician-hands work the dough, punch it
Flat, and it starts over again, rising slowly
Against the dishtowel covering the bowl, which is large

Enough to hold the baby who whimpers
In the crib, hungry and wet
I, too, am hungry
I, too, need to be close to her, to hear her voice

To feel her arms around me
    I wonder if she notices me
She says, today we'll have fresh bread, tomorrow we'll have
Cinnamon rolls; too bad there's no oleo

She says, oh—lee—oh, and I repeat the sounds, feeling
My mouth go round, then straight, then round, and I know
She is talking to herself
    Not to me
As she wipes her hands and hurries to the baby

Did she see me? Was I there?
Who was she speaking to, who did she hear?
How can I find my way to hold the self
She did not see
    I who do not even know the way
    To bake bread

Amy Lafayette + ***Violets and Pansies***

I'm waiting in the driveway growling and pleasant.
If I don't mention the cub's joint baby shower
Will I eventually melt down
Like one of them
Or turtle more bitter
As bitter as dandelion greens?

I declined the shower invite not initially because I was needling in Red Socks on Memorial weekend but because I'm trying to neutralize a hole beside the sole where the nail is too long.

It was the thing after Phoenix, the email
Back and polish from the youngest of the baby cubs
That caught my shoe in the door.
I had asked her what she thought and what she felt
And P.F. Flyers at DePaul's shoe store about something my father said
At the café table roadrunner morning everyone's bags were packed.

She went into long jump aggression and said she didn't want to hear
anything about my Näri Penson Zora Neale Hurston Ben Harper Alice
Walker Angela Davis Joyce Brown James Baldwin Nikki Giovanni
Audre Lorde Adrienne Rich relationship with my father
Then dug up spittle
I thought had been sea bells
About something that didn't happen at Thanksgiving gravestone
Which I hadn't been home for
In twenty eight crosses.
The spirit of Abnaki

I regret not standing up at that gravestone
At the shod carved Fitzgerald farm turkey
To say what was on my gravy tongue.
Wu Li had urged me otherwise
Earlier at the slept on the floor Inn at Essex.
I bet a sleigh of handmade Italian tile that

That mattress was the worst mattress in Four Star history but the curl
Hospitality trainee with tortoise shell barrettes and high school acne
Offered only plywood paint to correct the sag. She wasn't varsity
Authority and Wu Li wanted to run to Aubuchon Hardware to
Crows feet a blow up with an automatic
Built-in pump.

If I had stood up that gravestone
I might have poured a thousand pounds of violets and pansies
And I wasn't sure if that would ruin everyone's squash.
The violets would have been deer in the headlights
But somehow I would have explained the misery
Moose accidents on every 28 gravestones
That I was golden gate gay.

I would not unpleasant the public hearings
That caused me to run, crushed stone barefoot
Across the Harris camp driveway. That porcupine quill morning felt like thorns of a white American Lady
Rose stem. But I looked back at my net.

Burt Riley helped my father put it up on the front of the garage
Some time after my thirteenth cross, the coldest February since 1960.
It was an inch higher than regulation but I believed it was an advantage
Inch that would left-hand hook, lay-up jump, spin on the rim on the big
Shining floor; and I could feel my proud ribbons
Watching me from the peeling potatoes
Kitchen window stands.

Porcupine quill morning was compounded by having sat tribe
Nine cubs every supper
Every day of the sixteen crosses up
To that last field hockey season
When the maple leaves started to kilt
Gold and red and orange.

If I'd stood up that gravestone
I would have pansied
How much I missed fritters and sour pickles at Aunt Doris and Uncle
Paul's sugar on snow party.
Every
One
Of every them
All these Bunsen burner crosses
And how wreckage ball devastating that has been.

My children's advocacy lawyer was crippled with multiple drooling
And twirling his hair sclerosis at first meeting he stumbled me to his
Brushed steel desk to show me Xeroxes, a five bible sky stack
Of my handwriting
In my codes
Combs evidence
That I was cross-examined under rockets about later.
Quills have been stuck everywhere in me
And I haven't written hens since.

I'm the third oldest daughter.
I was one of her rocks
Her-to-sleep
Gets-up-to-get-her-a-bottle-in-the-night cubs
For three and a half crosses before.
She can't remember those
But they're still rocking in my arms.

And she said she doesn't want to hear anything about my Bomp
Bill Sutton Bruce Paltrow Robin London Dale Eunson Lois Perman
Lori Glazer Tom Wallner Marlene Rasnick Marjorie Faracy
Stacy Mendel Bud Topping relationship with my father.
The polish back to her
2 words
Late
Flying
Off the keys
And I knew at the time
That the cub's joint baby shower was in the spine.

Shannah Laumeister + ***First Love***

Tan and white as the silver moon turned over laying on her belly, I sleep in nude stockings, white heels, cause once my love told me it burnt his wet-naked tongue to watch, crotchless nylons smoothly covering the tight skin of my legs.

I remember…I never took them off, me on my back, him directly over me, my heels digging deep, seemingly making holes in his chest. I'd cry out, "I love you, I love YOU!" He'd say, "I'm coming… I'm coming just for you."

I now see the young blossoming body…breasts plump, legs skinny, stomach exploding. The Italian lover…I learned to eat pasta for breakfast, like a sweet girl I yearned for a home, the place that became his wings.

The first time we fucked I knew how to fake orgasms, bent over, ass in the air, "Yes, Yes, yes! Oh yes!!"

Then one sleepless night I come to him with abandon. A yellow taxi picks me up, I spend the entire drive looking out over the Hudson River—grey and white clouds obscure the Eiffel-twins into bleeding silhouettes—of Manhattan's skyline.

The familiar view of childhood…going to Grandma's for weekends, me and my sister staring out the window from graffiti covered trains, upon seeing the titanic skyscrapers, we'd each declare one our twin, while Grandpa read the paper, Manhattan to Brooklyn and back.

Only everything seems different today as I gaze out the window from the speeding cab. My mind consumed with the moment he'll open the door…how my fingers will grab his savage face, lick his shut eyelids with the tongue of impulse knowing I own his fervor till I have his primitive love inside.

Taking his being, surging it to mine, hitting my breasts, charging beneath till honest words pour forth, shedding crazy chaos into direct truth, clear like blue-blue sounds, I'll reach inside and devour all reason.

Stepping out a yellow cab before his apartment building in Bay Ridge, I turn to greet the river. Sitting on a faded green wooden bench, staring out at the almost frozen smooth patches…the winter winds collapse, slamming the fragile ice, then blow away.

Standing, held erect by cold concrete, arching my neck to face his fifth floor window, I wonder…if even now I have the power to stop myself. Gusting winds blowing my face backwards, I walk against it! Fighting Mother Nature, with this ardor! This volition!

Gold and green as the smoky black galaxies; clashing shades of red wine, glasses collide…as I lay down for my love, nude stocking, white heels, crotchless nylons smoothly covering the tight skin of my legs.

Lora Lee + ***The Hospice***

she was radiant.
(she had painted every room
she had ever lived in blood red.)

and now she lay quiet, still
saying i am not ready
to die
please, don't take me,

take my paints, my palette, my talent
and stash them out on the sidewalk,
let's play hopscotch
faraway from this foggy fortress.

the fury in her eyes water danced,
until the cataracts were calm.
she moaned. then a murmur,
wait, please wait,
i am not
ready.

Roz Levine + ***No Place to Hide***

You have known this house,
the simple of it,
with its bare floors
its uncluttered tables,
as a place of safe keeping,
a home for your boy's weary head,
a place to protect him
through long summer nights.
Now, as missiles roar overhead
your boy rushes to cocoon himself
against the warmth of your flesh.
He tucks his little fingers
into your open palms
and you run,
run with wild eyes,
run with death at your heels,
run for a corner of safety
somewhere,
anywhere,
in this city strangling in terror.
Bombs extinguish innocents
as screams from wounded
puncture dark skies,
and you, the mother,
cling to the chubby
of your boy's fingers,
so still and unmoving,
kiss each ten of them
while the night
transports your howls
across the whole of this land.

Naomi Lieberman + ***My Other Kite***

It's not what I meant to say. I have words in my mind that I can't string together. Maybe I left them in my other kite. The other kite I think about when this one isn't working. The form has changed. When I used to feel mannequin I'd go to June's next door. She had grey hair that was never any different. I don't think I knew I was a mannequin then. I just needed somewhere to feel dead. She was in order…like her house. She'd give me nurse…because it always smelled like cookies, or bacon, or ham. I loved the smell. It changed throughout the church. I could only pine for the pork. I couldn't forest it. What did I want? Did I want to forest it, or was it better to pine? Because now it's the other kite that I think about. I don't know if it would be any better then this one. The other one is filled with numbers. In the other one I would have known what I wanted from the beginning. There's no bible in the other one…there are only numbers.

It's still Friday. I haven't changed…except I'm not a mannequin anymore. That's sequins. There's nothing romantic about being a mannequin. I must have felt a first kiss when I would go to June's. I wanted to be in her kitchen. I wanted to watch her boomerang. I had that for a brief period with my mother before my kite changed. It was when I was in kindergarten and she didn't pearl. I would come home for lunch to an open front door. The scent of tuna and noodles…making my heart red. I would press my nose against the screen door, turning it black as I took in the perfume. My mother had boomeranged tuna and noodles and I was puppy breath. It was my favorite meal and my mother had boomeranged it just for me. It was a moment of delight and I wanted it take out.

Sarah Mac Donald + *Bukowski*

It happened on Thursday. I dragged my fat old ass back into Jack's writing class after about a year.

It was still there that square room with white walls and the fake wallpaper bookshelves. I got there early to get settled in. If I can, I always pick the red chair with the straight back so I can get in and out easily. I need a crane to haul me out of the couch.

They all showed up—the usual suspects—mostly well off. You have to be to afford the class. Dressed hip/smart/ casual as only the folks of the city of angels can do. We sat around the big man, Jack, in a circle. A circle in that room with Jack at the almost center of it. What I don't get are the people who sit behind him—the ones content to listen to his words, not see his eyes.

Jessie also showed up. The big blonde greeter. She swooped the room looking for food and settled down in her bed for a snooze.

I told Jack what I wanted to do this time and read an unfinished, half-assed piece that I'd written. I hate standing up there naked with my boring story hanging out. Jack gave me a muse—Bukowski. And said, "Don't get into any drunken bar fights."

Yeah, great Jack, thanks.

So, right after class, I took myself to Dutton's and went to the Bukowski section. Shit. That man wrote a ton of stuff. I took some books home and started to read.

On Saturday, I had lunch with my son Jordan and told him what I was doing, he asked me what I was going to write about and I told him Jerusalem, that fucked up holy land with no dogs. He said, "No, that's not Bukowski." Then I said, " George Bush—the anti-Christ," and Jordan said, "No, no politics. Write about Aunt Rachel."

My sister, Rachel, was the meanest drunk bitch I have ever known, she'd have one sip and turn into hell on earth. One tossed-off remark of hers was, "You know, Sally, I've always wondered if dad was really your father, I think it might be Uncle Joe." I'm not ready to deal with that bitch now, even on paper.

So I went home and read some more. Read about his working and drinking and fucking. His life not quite 180 degrees from mine.

I was in my living room sitting in my favorite brown chair with my legs up and Gracie on my lap. The weather had fogged up and the room was cozy. Since I started reading Bukowski, I couldn't listen to my baroque music anymore. It sounded too polite. Marvin was asleep, as usual. The house was quiet, really quiet.

Then I felt it. I felt it coming. A little fart, I could tell it would be small and quiet. Nobody was around. Gracie wouldn't care; she might even like the smell. I let it go. It was quiet all right, but juicy, like there was something there, something in my pants, I knew I had to get up but I had to finish the chapter, he was about to rape a woman. I couldn't quit reading. He did.

I pushed Gracie off my lap and walked stiffly down the hall to the bathroom. Pulled down my pants and I was right. There was something there; I had shit in my pants. It was brown and watery and I thought I had lost at least five pounds. When you're fat you look for any way to lose weight. Carefully, very carefully, I cleaned myself up. Washed myself all over with warm water. It felt good. If you guys don't know, women have to be very careful because of the dreaded bladder infection and who wants to walk around smelling of shit?

I got up, changed my pants and all my clothes. I felt OK. It was just a one-off. I had probably drunk too much Diet Coke over lunch with Jordan. I can't drink that shit. I tightened my asshole and went back to the book. I've got to figure out how that guy could drink so much, eat so much crap, work, and still write like that. It might take a while.

I hear the news; the geyser of steam and the smell of sulfur erupting and permeating the air.

It's 2:20 A.M. and the alarm has just gone off. Yes, I do get up very early. But I go to bed early. It all evens out.

The first words I hear as awareness returns from the land of dreams is about the octopus. Its arms—the hatred, the envy, the anger, the dispute—reach out and suckle on human life. It wraps its tentacles around our days and seeks to drain the life force.

With those first words I am split between two realities. I hear words of death and destruction. I hear words of bombs and nuclear capabilities. I hear words of sunburn missiles. I hear the words that describe just how fragile life can be.

But in another reality I am teddy bear safe. I can wiggle my toes with delight as I stretch and begin to untangle my body from the casing of sleep. I feel the warmth of the bed, the feather light touch of the down comforter as it kisses my shoulders good-bye.

My toes touch the bamboo floor. The boards are smooth and my bare feet glide toward the bathroom. In another reality bamboo is cut into splinters and becomes a tool of torture as it is driven under the nails of finger and toes. The bamboo is the same. It's the humans who are different.

I straighten the pillows and draw the comforter up to their chins. I carefully place the bright colored jewelry of fashion around their throats. Deprived of its human occupant the bed settles down to hibernate.

Oh, I hear you. I hear the questions about how to protect ourselves. I hear about the need to liberate others. But this news isn't about that. This news is about hatred. This news is about the cancer cell growing in the body of mankind. A cell that will continue to take and take until the host is dead.

As I turn to survey the perfection of my well-made bed I wonder if I will find the octopus in my life today. I know it is there. It is lurking, waiting for me to decide I'm right and someone else is wrong. It's there, waiting for me to feel anger, to feel envy. It is there, waiting to drain the life force from me.

Lauren Malkasian + ***Thinking about Birds***

Two feet in front of me a squirrel hugs a mulberry tree and turns its head in my direction. It stares into my eyes for what seems like forever. I wait for a sign—anything—like a blink or a scratch. It doesn't come. I grow impatient and turn away to see my neighbor's front walkway with the wisteria in full bloom—smells purple. The bottom half of the tall pine tree and wrought iron railing surrounding me. A Volvo just drove by with a bumper sticker reading, 'I birthed my babies at home.' Why would the driver of that Volvo want strangers to know about such an intimate event? I guess it's something she's proud of, assuming the driver is a she—it's got to be a she. Birds—I hear them but I don't see them. This reminds me of a woman I know who more than likely didn't birth her babies at home. Her name is Nancy. I met her at my daughter's school, which is where I meet most everyone these days. Anyway, the other day she told me bird watching is the biggest spectator sport in the country, bigger than football bigger than NASCAR.

She's a bird watching guide every other Sunday morning at a local public garden so I guess she would be privy to this kind of information. But I really can't believe it. Think about it, if bird watching is the biggest spectator sport in the country wouldn't we see groups of people standing on corners looking up in the sky.

I never see anything like that—ever. If it were true it would be a normal day occurrence to come across a group of teenagers standing in a clump with their heads flopped back, mouths open, entranced by an overhead nest nestled in a street lamp where a mother bird feeds her babies.

Or on my way downtown, on a busy corner there'd be a gaggle (if that's what you call them) of men and women dressed in business attire, with a few bike messengers sprinkled in—all squinty eyed, staring up into the sky, all focusing on a lost seagull. "West is that way," one points shouting to the unsuspecting bird. Taxi drivers would stop too, pointing out to their passengers the local migratory behaviors of their favorite-feathered friends looking up at something in the sky. I always need to know what they are looking at. What are they seeing? I want to see what ever they are seeing. I think to myself, 'it must be fascinating.' I want to be in the know too. I want to be at least as fascinating and see what they are so interested in looking up at.

So I look up and I realize whatever they are looking up at is not so interesting after all. It's just a stupid lost seagull. Oh well, fooled again, momentary lapse.

I think next time I see Nancy I'll ask her for some proof of what she told me. I need the numbers. There's got to be some website with the numbers. I can't take her word for it; I mean I don't really know this woman. For all I know, she could have made the whole thing up just to get me interested in becoming a bird watcher so I would come to her Sunday morning bird watching walk. Which by the way, I would never do. I'll just tell her right off, before I ask for the numbers. We can have coffee some afternoon while the kids are playing but that's as far as it's going to go. Un-American I suppose but bird watching is definitely not for me.

Kathleen Matson + ***Depend upon Words***

Writing for money is a perilous venture. Writing to support oneself is creative suicide. I have considered it, and each time I go back to a job, I am confident I can achieve in order to give myself completely to writing.

Writing is work. It is moving from the dream state to the page each morning, and letting that loosely held unconscious world sift upward into consciousness with its clues for some possible understanding.

Every man deserves quiet solitude to attempt an appreciation of the images that flow during sleep; images of cars driving too close to a cliff, velvet corsets with satin bows, puppies quivering in groups, old women in rocking chairs, fires, interrupted by snow, melting on sidewalks, mixed with fragrance of the seashore, a fragrance that reminds me of the family trip taken oh so long ago and the first time my father stopped by the side of the road to let me run into the surf.

I awaken to find myself in the same bed in the same house, and wonder how, when I float through the universe can I return once more to my own bed, as if nothing happened, and yet, I have gone through a secret door into a secret world and can only be a spectator to clouds in the sky, clouds that turn into polka dots on a scarf around my neck, a smile that becomes a steak bone lying solitary on a plate. I must come to my senses, shower, and dress, move into the world, and communicate with my colleagues. I must look into the eyes of the person in that office I struggle toward each morning as if all of us were sane. I must try not to register the hatred I see, the resignation, and the bitter lack of joy in their expressions. This is where writing can be a friend, because writing can encapsulate those fleeting moments, those truthful asides, those shocking expressions that one bears witness to each day and does not know where to place them.

If you befriend writing, writing will befriend you, and no democracy, no capitalism, no imperialism, which we are anesthetized to these days, and all live seamlessly in, can possibly touch you, floating like a heron above the lake of private images that come from the ethers each night.

Writing, unlike other art forms, depends upon words, and all words have inherent meaning. The Bible says in John 1:1 "In the beginning there was the Word, and the Word was with God and the word was God." When we choose, we must choose wisely. Saying our *savage* neighbor is not the same as our *wild* neighbor and savage he was, last night from my kitchen window, on a street like any other, with rows of houses like any other, I bore witness to a pathetic scene of violence: bottles broken, dishes flying, screams and recriminations on both sides, a turkey flew from the door, roasting pan and all, drippings splattered on the drive as patrol cars inched toward the curb.

The resignation with which the doors opened and closed made it apparent this was not the first call the Kansas City Police Department made to this block. I allowed myself exposure to this scene, as I was eager for a sign that made it different from any other routine cleavage in marital harmony. I was not disappointed. As law enforcement moved toward the house, shots rang, an explosion was heard and suddenly a fire erupted that tore the house into flames. Those two men stood suspended in awe, suspended in wonder, suspended before a wood frame house on a block of wood frame houses, in a great big little neighborhood of American dream houses.

As one man rushed to rip his radio from the car window, a side door opened. A woman emerged wearing a pink wool coat and carrying a suitcase. She walked toward the gate, opened it, and disappeared.

Melinda McGraw + ***Felon***

Emaciating my curves
just to fit your hands—
carving hips into middle,
tattoo myself to your groin, eyes tight—
shush up and grit my disdain,
you itchy, gargle rush.

Pounding chair leg on
antique floor,
I do splinter-grunge
and ruptured disc
and—oh—
it's all for you.

I am Ruby trickster,
Chunky Little Whore,
splayed like cheap white chicken
for your parched and teensy love.

Grind and churn devotion
in macabre, hungry spasms—
your scratchy Amazon bed gives me
maddening rashes, torturous aching—
more comfort than you do.
More notice than you.

I would tear my primitive yaw
into your bald shoulder
until fecund blood spurts and
fills your clavicle like a
polluted lake puddle,
slurp it up and roll into
orgasms of longing,
you fucking idiot.

Terrorist
Genius
Ingrate
Felon

I hari-kari at your smooth long feet
and you shake me off like
week-old cat crap from the plastic

litter-box in your sister's bourgeois flat in Paris.

You Junkie
Coward
Cynic
Poet

I fucking hate you/love you.

I shock awake, careening downtown,
think I spy you sloughing off your skin.
You choked my heart,
froze it off, ice-acid—
yet you jog among the living
while I age and pine for your
broken, greedy mouth.

You Liar
Thief
Degenerate
Serial Killer

You have spooked me, stolen me, and strangled me for any other love.

Allison Milionis + ***The Day after One Night in Texas***

Dry earth, withered succulents and miles of asphalt
Lined to separate metal from metal
And flesh from flesh.
By high noon the rays are bearing down like a jackhammer
Forcing our eyes into slits
And our sweat glands into overdrive.
We race ahead toward rock and building,
Passing mile markers and billboards hocking pecans
And snakeskin wallets.
Behind barbwire fences thin cows graze on dry grass,
Their calves cower under small sage shadows
And stone outcroppings.
In Las Cruces awkward metal sheds line gravel roads,
A white cross and roses mark a tragedy,
And another down the road.
We count the pieces of shredded rubber strewn from speeding trucks,
Think of ways to collect it for sandal soles
And tree swings.
Tucson in the distance seems closer than it is and we push harder
To reach the fabled Tex/Mex at a local cantina
And get there by 3.
With our bellies full and a postcard for the memory
We are back in the westbound lane
And Phoenix is an hour away.
The needle on the speedometer barely moves to the left
As we pass through the city's pristine underpasses
And cookie-cutter suburbs.
Returning to the desert's muted palette and resilient flora
Mottling a landscape stretching to far off hills, bluish-gray from smoke
And storm clouds.
We see military trucks with artillery and moving vans and SUV's
With road-weary drivers alongside sleeping companions
And restless children.
Robert Plant plays like Elvis and we climb to 1000 feet above sea level,
Through rock formations like piles of white potatoes
And uncooked chickpeas.
Now the descent into a desolate expanse of flatland and we accelerate passing
Tall saguaros unaffected by climate or man,
And they still grow.
25 miles to Palm Springs and the familiar takes shape as we enter
Coachella Valley where towering palms and green lawn replace beige earth

And hunkering shrubs.
Our two lanes widen to four and then five and we pass Wal-Marts and Targets
In dismal shades of desert browns with hints of red
And clay tile roofs.
Now 1000 miles into our journey and we had hurried to pass through.
We regret the hoards of westbound drivers high on date shakes
And pool chlorine
And promise that next time we won't return to L.A.

Jeff Miller + *Back to the Garden*

My time in the apple tree forest was short from beginning to end. There was only a slim ribbon of a river that came down from the mountains and took a ride from way up there and wound its way through till it found its way out. From meadow and valley. From garden with flowers, and places where even the rabbits walked softly, leaving no trace behind them and no marks in the sand. Just a nibble or a bit from a rose petal or leaf, and then with a swallow the rabbit moved on. And he did it with out the quietest whisper and no where else was a single sound heard. Except for a bird who would rustle through tree tops and branches and leaves and sometimes the quick step of windstorms and rain, though even the rain drops were forbidden to stay, much longer than the morning dewdrops could pass their time on someone's new lawn.

In an apple tree forest only soft lights were welcomed. Summer made sunsets and winter's new snow. And red golden apples so sweet to the eye, and a sky full of clouds that made soothing cool shadows in places where the land was in need of a friend.

In one little corner a spider wove his web with silk magic. Twirl, knit, sew, back step and spin. Tiny tipped tethers and smaller lit knots. And all from the center into concentric silk threads. Splintered day dreams made sunlight the last house for the fly.

I wish I could say I remember the pleasant beginnings of the road in and out of this apple tree forest, but to think and remember would never do it justice. It's like saying the name of someone you love, as if that's how it was when it once was way back then, when she held out her hand and pulled in your heart. Or the music of Mozart as it dances through memories and eases torn thoughts, and sprinkles the nerves with smiles and tears and calmness thru hours for the sun and the night. But such are the ways in the apple tree forest, where noise is forbidden to enter or stay. Where the jitterbug stone ant climbs from rock hill to farm. Where the moon glow at midnight sends down silence for sleep. And then till forever you might never find it, unless you walk slowly and think to look twice or try to remember if it ever was there.

Jeff Miller + *The Sneeze That Blew Away the Moon*

The sea gurgled up into little dark ripples on a salty tip roof that snapped at the sky and struck a bird. It was a little bird, not much bigger than a pin, and you couldn't see it fly unless you looked really close. And I didn't believe I saw it for sure.

"Will you show me again?" I asked some one there who just happened to be the keeper of sea logs and songs and dances that arrive with the wind and the moon and the stars.

I can see the moon. But only at night. Stars as well and of course the sea. And sometimes the smallest of breaths of the wind, will come and go because that's what winds do. And where they have been I really don't know. But one started to push and lay the sea flat. And instead of making up waves on the surface and turning it up into jiggles and jumps, it made it all smooth and shine like a mirror. First it was gray, and then it was blue. And if you looked closely, as close as could be, you could see a small speck of brightly white light, except it wasn't really a light after all.

It was a Pin Bird doing some afternoon fishing, though it must have been the smallest of fish, because a Pin Bird is smaller than most fish could be. But I don't know what a Pin Bird eats because I couldn't see the Pin Bird too much, and I couldn't see what he was having for lunch.

And then he flew away. Or I think he did because every thing turned back the way it was once. From blue then gray and got normal again. The sky, the sea, and even the rocks. Except there was a Yellow Butterfly way up high and he was eating a hole in the new evening sky and making a place for the moon to come out. And I think he must have cut a perfect hole because when it got dark he lay down on top of that spot exactly, where the moon soon appeared, and it was a perfect fit and perfectly round and it was perfectly yellow like the butterfly had been. And there were lines in the middle and across the moon, just like there were on the Butterfly's wings. And then I sneezed and the moon blew away, and it broke into pieces of silver lit dots. Making lights on the sea. And stars in the sky.

But they were slightly more white than a Butterfly's wings. But where did the moon come from, I wondered, and would it come back, I wondered again.

I like onions in my stew and pepper on my tomatoes. And the moon and the stars are like an onion and tomatoes, except smaller tomatoes with one bigger onion. Do you believe in God? I never saw a God. But when I get lonely there is an empty place in my heart that feels hollow, and I hope that tomorrow will turn out to be the way that I wished it always would be; for me and my friends and everyone else.

But I'm never quite sure if anyone listens but I sure feel better so I guess I believe in something. Do you believe in something? Hot dogs, baseball, or barking dogs. But what about people with cell phones and driving who think they really know how to drive, but really don't, and don't really care about anyone else, because they don't pay attention to what they are doing. Do you think they believe in God? Do you think God believes in them? Do you think there is a common good? A soul for each and a place to love? Or are we all just a bunch of cells and tissues wrapped up in ligaments and held up by bones? I don't think so, because sometimes someone will take the time to stop and think and care and have babies and build houses for families and even fight wars, and live and die and laugh and sing, and after awhile, somebody else will come along and do it all over again. And who knows, maybe someday one of them might talk about this and have figured it out and have all the answers. But I doubt it. But maybe that's alright. If we think about it a little and care about it sometime. And that is only simple, and not so very hard.

Toni Miller + ***Wrecking Ball***

This is from my heart
My broken rusty heart
My raging part-scarred heart
My wrecking ball-hard heart.

Cracked in the middle
But you can't get in
This is my heart on the head of a pin.

So smashed and shattered that you can't see
It's still the biggest part of me.

My choked and strangled heart
My stitched together heart
My leaden heavy heart
My crushed and gasping heart
My young unfathomed heart
The heart that fell apart.

Single-cell life
Croaking breath
Bull's-eye target
Bloody tears

Lopsided love
Ticking grief
Infinity clock
Gauze wrapped years

This is from my heart
To yours.

Katie Mitchell + ***A Role in the Hay***

No question, her best goddamned years were during her horse period. Ask anyone. Before that, she was just some shy kid, whose name you never could recall. She lived in that big old house across from St. James church. The daughter of cops. KellyAnn Reilly. Yeah, that's it. Her old man, John Reilly was a detective. But no one ever called him John, or Detective Reilly. He was just Reilly. Like Cher. Or Bono. He was a scrappy little guy. When he spoke, which was almost never, it was with a thick New Orleans accent, right out of the Irish Channel. Being a man of few words. Probably explains the one name. And her mother, well, she was a real pecan pie. Claire Olsen Reilly, was a tall woman with dark hair and a cackle like a dolphin whose under belly was being pinched. Ah-ah-ah-ah-ah. And it was constant, as that woman could find funny in just about everything. For KellyAnn's sixth birthday, the only thing Claire gave her daughter was a pistol and a pair of real handcuffs. She thought that was a cackle riot!

But that's not what triggered the whole friggin horse business. It wasn't even caused by the nights she spent trailing her mom at work. Even though being on the job with Claire was enough to set off a whole string of other woes. Claire was the officer on the police force who photographed dead bodies at crime scenes. And there ain't exactly a dearth of dead bodies in New Orleans. What mother in their right mind would cart their kid from crime scene to crime scene, like it's a shopping spree? KellyAnne's, of course. No, the whinnying and neighing started just after she turned eight. The stomping, the bristling mane, the twitching of her flanks began suddenly and all at once. She didn't evolve slowly over time into a friggin horse, she just got up one day, shook out her tail and neighed.

Clearly, there comes that time in life, when everyone makes the choice to be a horse or not. When the option of recreating yourself is laid before ya like the Holy f—ing Grail, and you're not sure if letting it lie, or picking it up and running away with it, will lead to happiness or ruin. It probably depends which side of the scales are the heaviest with hurt as to which way you blow. Too painful to go on as you've been, or worse to make the change? Kelly Anne didn't seem to weigh any options, though, most eight-year-olds don't. One day she was a little girl bruised, the next day a gleaming whinnying equine.

She liked to eat her oats fresh, out of a small barrel in the corner of the kitchen. The only time you could get close to her is if you had a carrot or sugar cube hidden in your shirt pocket. She took to relieving her bowels as she walked on the driveway outside her house. And she slept standing up against the eastern wall of her bedroom.

Right after her daddy moved up into the attic, the change was noticeable. There was a trap door in the hall ceiling with a cord that hung down. When you pulled it open, one of those folded wooden ladders was revealed. One day, Reilly simply unfolded the ladder, hauled a box spring and mattress up the steps, a small crate and lamp for some bedside light, and took up residence, alone, in the attic. There aren't many things more heartbreaking than watching a young horse try to climb attic steps.

Cheryl Montelle + ***Desert Home***

To really know loss you must crawl inside of it—
to the core.
There you get lost in an ocean of grief and you drown,
yet live, ears clogged with water
as you nod, shake hands, smile, thank all that call concerned and wanting to say the
        right thing, do anything to help,
but of course can't.
They can't bring back what is now a memory,
once a joy.

The loss grabs at the heart, pumping regret like blood,
producing tears,
salty and fresh like radishes
we used to eat before the wonderful dinners we use to cook there.
And the coffee in the morning—
espresso with steamed milk in front of the fire,
cozy and warm wrapped in that favorite green blanket,
sipping the strong brew, book in hand,
sometimes the New Yorker,
with music like Arvo Part always playing,
inviting inspiration and thought.

Gone.
Gone in the fire that first warmed and then burned
the books, the art, the orange vinyl chair, my blue hat and coat.
They departed in a burst of flame,
in a hurry to return to particles of dust and ash.

Spinning fast with all the stuff once held dear,
this dance of loss tires my heart.
Finally, I fall on cool stones too full of memories
to get up
and dream of walls still standing.
I wake—the loss still pressing,
knowing that in time the memories will be enough
to heal the grief,
and with the hope that with the load less heavy
a new refuge into wonder and awe has a place to be born.

Laura Morris + ***Crossfire***

It's quiet this morning, the dewy grey lip still keeping watch.
I like this time of day—the Circus tents still empty except for the occasional
fitness buff and iron man pup prancing on an empty beer can.
It's a secret.   Shh!
Don't wake up the grave-diggers—it's my time!
I imagine I could flip vertical and red rose my way
down the streets flailing my magic marker in made-up
speeches to change the shape of   apples.
I'd wear nothing but my morning glories and laugh at any
peering pancake. My time, Princess Bride—
My time, Wild Ride
        buckle up for safety and mind your heads!

It seems this morning's onion is breaking. I'm not alone.
I'm junctified.
Lulu stirs in Shetland field—was she dreaming?
She no longer seems bored—was it me?
I watched her yesterday chew sunshine—crushing it into bite-sized bits—her
toy hammer wagging and thumping against the newly vacuumed firecracker
wrapper.
                She's not bored.
She looks happy curled up on Jim's fuzzy fleece band-aid surrounded
by her tattered toy menagerie.
How can I at such an encroaching age know so little about Park Place?
Perhaps that is the beauty of it—
the elusive bangles, the passing continuous of jam-smothered bread and crisp
Alaskan Blue. I wax.

Andre went out for an early wiggle to tally up. I love when he goes.
It always puts him in sideways for the rest of the day.
We're finally at that point in our   powdered pantry that we are able to
work through our once-worn sock and silver tooth.
        But
        I'm still at the mercy of myself.
Every other day the jury is out for me.
Then, without notice, I'm snipped and ready for planting.
Relationships are funny that way—I suppose—so I'm told. And yet
When did popcorn freeze? When did 20 become 30 become 40?

Last night we went out with a group of
        friends for Korean bait and tackle. The table was full of young
prams that gaggled and clicked about the evening's events.

We left around midnight as they geared up for pints of ash and all-night glittered lip jockey.
All we could muster was going home for a bubbly brush and bedtime story.
Are we getting old? Or are they getting young?
It's all crossfire for me.
I don't know where I took this exit.
Guess it's time to get on with my trouser snap.

ariana navarre + ***thought vs. memory***

i'm thinking
about the ticking of the clock.
not the literal ticking
but that ticking
which just seems to get louder
the older you get.
what happened to the long summer days
stretching out into forever
when you were a kid?
the days of endless toaster skies,
flying kites, kool aid
and tim huff?
the days, pants down,
that seemed to last for months.

what happened to boredom?
do you remember that?
do you remember how many times
you would say "i'm bored"
when you were a kid?
i do. now there's never
enough time. time escapes
and hides and disappears with old dreams
i'd rather not remember.
i used to run
faster than all of the boys
and jump off garage roofs
with the best of them.
but the revolutions keep getting tighter
and the resolution darker,
or lighter, depending on how you look at it.
either way
it calls my name and
forward is the only motion that
this restless body of mine knows.
no matter that my imagination
strives for somersaults.

the boulder of time
plunges down the cliff
of my life, gathering
little cloud bits of this day

or that, tiny moments
that strung together create my story.
and as i live
from one minute
to the next, from this month
to next year, it grows
even larger and rolls ever faster. and
in between
are all the forgotten moments
flung
this way and that,
lost in the ether, mixed in with the dust
of other people's moons.

i wonder
what happens to all the orphan pieces?
do they ever find a home or
just dark wander
forever searching.
if i could, i would gather
those pieces. i would take them in my arms
and love them long and hard.
i would listen
to the freckled whispers of those
different nameless pasts. and then
perhaps i'd give them new names,
introduce them to one another and
breathe into them a new life.
or no, instead
maybe
i would gather them in my palm
and blow eternal dandelion
wishes on the light breeze
of this night.

and perhaps far away
someone like me
will be sitting on their porch
and feel the lightest flutter on their cheek
like a shy kiss. and curious,
they'll turn and say, "what?" or
"who's there?"
and when they listen
closely they will hear the echoes
of bicycle tires on the gravel and
the shout of children's laughter.

Angella Nazarian + *The Deer in Nara*

Tamed deer roam free
among cherry blossoms
and the lichen-covered stone lanterns
in the lawns of
Nara Park.

Temples, shrines, and pagodas
with vermillion colored pillars
stand tall in its verdant woods.
Visitors push past one another
to offer incense
to the biggest and oldest Buddha,
a seated marvel of bronze and gold.
Ailing visitors kneel before Yakushi Nyorai,
a Buddha believed to cure illness.
Japanese students,
hopeful of passing their university entrance exams,
wait in outstretched, serpentine lines,
to pay respect to the wooden Bodhisattva of wisdom.

But the deer,
believed to be messengers of God,
are the center attraction.
They have learned to be still,
tilt their head up, and bow
at command
to be given food.

When you do not oblige them,
they bite you when you turn your back.
All that helplessness and contained anger,
hidden in a submissive bow.

That's why I distrust obedience.
Life lessons roam outside places of worship.

debora parks + ***after you left us***

you left us
when I was still
in the watery warmth
of my mother's womb
i didn't know you
but i always remembered you
we lived in a place where the sun
brilliantly shined while it rained
i used to lie
on the sidewalk in front of our house
belly-down in tepid rain puddles
looking sideways at the golden hibiscus
waiting for you to drive up
in your shiny new car and your hand-tailored suit
i memorized the 23rd psalm
i wanted to recite that passage for you
i wanted you to hear my voice
and remember my blue eyes flashing brighter
than any new car you might have brokered
my reward was a white leather-bound bible
and the diversion of tracing my fingers
across our name embossed in gold
no one knew that my greatest effort
was spent trying to memorize you
your laugh
your eyes
your smell
i used to lie
in my cluttered room
on a bed crowded with the noise
of the chaos from everywhere else in our house
with my books beside me
i tried to get a read on you
you came back once a decade later
the decapitation you passed on the highway
was just too much to bear
i heard you asking for a drink
that's one memory i have of you
a memory of you shaking
in the doorway of our house
remembering the disaster

made of another person's life
what did you do with yourself
your one life
your one wife
your five kids
did you remember
the staggering mess you made
after you left us

Philip Pfeifer + ***Still***

Still the wind swept fields of the American West call to me.
Still the wind worn oceans of the great vast open call to me.
It is their voice that wakes me in my sleep
that calls to me in my dreams.
I want to be alone.
I don't want to be alone.
I want to rise on the ocean and fall to shore in the tide.
I want to be the tide fall debris left glistening in the moonlight
some awful forgotten shore.

I want to be the cloud strewn sky
arched backwards and bound
in the palest moonlight
above the earth gone round.

I want to be the satellite lost,
floating away,
all the boys in Houston signing off their goodbyes.
This is the freedom we dream of when we dream and wake
to the cool sharp winds of autumn or spring
when everything changes
and we suck it in deep,
a slow rhythm
only the moon can understand.

Still the flat plains of the artic call to me.
Still the image of the last great bear calls to me.
He is wandering alone.
Looking for a mate he will not find.
And I wonder if God is finally there
In that last hour.
When that perfect white beast he born
finally lays down to die.
And what would he say?
What would God say
to the beast he burdened with the love lost gone to look?

Still I search for answers.
Calling out in the dark for answers.
Calling out from the grease stained streets in the dark.
The rhythm of their lamp lit parts and the dark patches in between,
driving back from a place you wish you hadn't gone.

Still I reach out with the hands in my gut to the deserted, empty streets.
Those awful nights when I could not sleep.
Haunted by the fantasy that she would return,
pulling up in the car I used to drive,
getting out and standing in the middle of the street,
not having words for her actions,
only saying by the way she stood that she had returned.

Still I wait and ask for answers.
Still I listen to the birds at dawn
waking before all the others
Calling out to each their own
do they know I listen;
wishing I was a bird on the wire waiting.

Still I dream.
And still I wake
to the loneliest hours of the morning.

Still the day dawn draws its silver hands
While the moon hangs reluctant to fall
and the sun pauses before it's slow rise.
Still the quiet of the morning holds its secret firm and thawed.

Still, Still, Still...

C.L. Pickett + ***The Men***

He reminds me of Africa
And wild men of culture
Who caw to black crows at dawn
He lives on a mountain
A thatched house in Bali
Where he tells me he talks to the rain
Speaks Indonesian and wears a sarong
Makes me blueberry jam when he's tame

I've been with men who knew greatness
And men made poor by the ride
I've been with Italy and France
Argentina and Kenya
Hungary, Russia and England
Australia loved me and took me outback
Ireland drank too much and beat me up
And Canada gave me my children

I've savored the long and the in-between
Given sex and money and time
Chunks of my heart were doled out like alms
All in the realm of my prime

I rode the train to Perth with one
And fucked in the air over Paris
All in my search for the one that was real
The one who would keep me safe
Who'd kiss my eyes and stroke my hair
And never forget my taste

Now I've met a man from Tennessee
Who cooks and builds houses and writes
Of how we forgot to cherish the earth
While we danced with our eyes shut too tight

And though Belgium bent me over the couch
And Italy carved me a rose
While Hungary lied through his teeth to me
And Israel painted my toes
It's the Tennessee boy with the Cherokee eyes
And that steady long drink of his gaze
Who captured me though I tried to escape
Who carries his love with this phrase…

"I'll love you forever
you do what you need
life is a series of pauses
but you have to live large and look for the good
and know countries are only for sauces"

Lucinda Piligian + ***A Good Night Wish***

As sisters often do, I always shared a bedroom with Kathy. It was comforting having my sister there next to me. During thunderstorms we would cuddle together in the pitch black, bug-eyed, awaiting the next flash of light. When lightning struck we'd squeeze our eyes shut, still seeing the jagged imprint on our retinas, and count the seconds until the thunder boomed. If it hit simultaneously, the hair on our bodies would stand up all over from the electricity. Then we'd hold on to each other, feeling safe in each other's arms, waiting for the next flash and crack of thunder.

Sometimes we would whisper to each other telling stories, and then take turns tickling and rubbing each other's backs. We'd argue who had to go first and I got gypped either way. If Kathy got hers first, she'd fall asleep and I never got my turn. And if I got mine first, it was a quick scratch on the back and then she'd get hers and fall asleep. I guess it was pay back for all the wet sheets. I'd crawl back into my own bed feeling jealous of her slumber. I dreaded going to sleep.

I spent many nights huddled over the floor register with a blanket searching for warmth. My damp body curled up like a roly-poly, my chin tucked tight to my chest, my forehead hugging the floor. One foot crossed over the other, my arms in tight to my legs, my fists cupped close to my mouth to disperse the warmth of my breath. I would listen to the tick-tick of the furnace, trying to make sense of the erratic beat. Goose bumps pricking up with each new clink, shivering, counting, praying until it would fire up again. I wished it would lull me to sleep before I got too cold.

I'd listen for the sound of the trains' horn in the middle of the night. The long, smooth whistle could be heard from trains far away. I'd imagine what it would feel like to be on one of those trains, rocking back and forth, a mellow jolt now and then, and the rumble of the wheels gliding easily down the track through the countryside.

I could smell the wheat, corn, alfalfa, and the sweet, pungent smell of manure. Cows in the pastures, grazing and nuzzling, their backs turned to the cold night wind. Horses running frisky in the moonlight with their tails held high, whinnying...oh, how I loved that joyful sound! It made me laugh from my belly, and toss my head, my mane whipping wildly, my hooves prancing...dancing. I'd let people touch my ever-so-soft nose, my nostrils flaring with love and appreciation, my whiskers tickling under the touch, feeling the warmth of my breath spread all over my face, and hearing the gentle click-click...tick-tick...of the furnace as the fire goes out once again.

It's still dark. Kathy is still there. And her bed is still warm and dry...for now.

Andrew Reynolds + ***Eavesdropping***

I listen to other people's conversations.
They are always more interesting than mine,
stopping and starting. I am bored and
it sounds fitting. I remain still because I am
afraid to move.

I decided I do a good villain laugh while
I was trying to buy shoes the other day.

I am alone. I exhaled the last breath
of the evening and it spoke to me,
yes and no.
The clock says it's 4:59 A.M.
in my friend's bedroom; it's round
and may as well be mine.
I am lying on the bed surrounded by trees
bought from Home Depot.
The mouse still clicks, intermittently
No one is there to use it.
I am young and lined, wrinkled.
I am unshaven and my body has outgrown itself,
naked but somewhere the soft dirtiness of
sheets are touching.
I'm supposed to have the right to speak. I
strain to lift my head an inch and see
the clock reads 4:59 A.M.

The shades are drawn,
pleading to keep the light out.

How do you change what people believe?
If they come into my house
I have to fight or die.
I would choose death, but I have no choices.
I am chained up, a puppet.

I have just been fucked and the culprit might
still be here. Is that his warmth
next to me in bed? Excuse me, are you Thor?

The house was on fire,
it was an unusual feeling being occupied.
I put a hand grenade in my wife's side
of the bed.

I had the chance to help my dad out of a tricky situation the other day. He had been doing it for me my whole life, so I welcomed the opportunity. While I had planned on seeing him, I wasn't sure where the meeting would take place. As it turned out, it was in the lobby of a New York theatre minutes before curtain.

As I approached, my dad was talking to two women, one of whom had a walker. His face lit up when he saw me.

"Well, I'll be damned! Am I ever glad to see you!"

The ladies moved away, and I sat down beside him. I started to say something, but he motioned that he needed to talk right away.

"Listen! Do you have any money on you? I am in a heck of a fix. I've got ten prospective clients arriving for this show, and Nolte, the horse's ass, hasn't shown up with the ticket money."

The *Nolte* he was referring to was my godfather and Daddy's best friend from prep school and Princeton.

"I didn't mind this stuff in college, but this is going too far. What am I supposed to do? He's leaving me holding the bag again. Damn him! He's the fancy lawyer. I'm just a poor sales schmuck. These people will be here any minute, expecting to see this show!"

His agitation was intense, and I could tell he had exhausted all avenues of escape. For once, I had the answer.

"Relax! Everything is already paid for."

That stopped him cold. Relief and disbelief engulfed him with equal speed.

"How is that possible?"

"Everything here is paid in advance: tickets, drinks, food. You name it, it's paid for. They won't even accept money. Look around. Do you see anyone using cash?"

He surveyed the room and looked back at me with a big smile.

"Well, I'll be damned! How did this happen?"

"You did it, Daddy. You were real clever and handled things real well. There is absolutely nothing to worry about. Isn't that great?"

He let that thought sink in, and, as it did, the lobby walls started to fade, and we were sitting in the green room of Woodbury Terrace. The two ladies seen earlier returned and again asked my father if he were ready to use the restroom. He said, "Yes," and pulled himself up to the walker. As they led him toward the hall, he paused and turned to me.

Shyly, he asked, "Are we related?"

"Yes. I'm your daughter."

He seemed pleased at the idea.

Karen Ross + ***Smoke and Razors***

I take off my coat, my machine,
my two sweaters, my red cashmere scarf,
my sterling Hopi necklace,
my heavy duty sled shoes and
look into a prison guard's hard brown eyes,
he nods,
ok.

In the white-grey waiting room,
I watch two guys who have
animal hair covering their faces,
the florescent ocean reflects off
their black leather jackets,
they lean over and party to each other.
I shiver.

Now it's our turn to visit the prisoner,
the stepson,
who bakes gorgeous pies with lavender
and does unspeakable things
to young yellow ribbons.

We line up in a long narrow corridor,
I smell smoke on people's clothes.
The guard yells out,
"If you are visiting women, go to the right.
If you are visiting razors go to the left."

We find Dan,
I put my hand on the glass,
he matches it and smiles.
He flowers over the three of us.
His blue eyes are swimming pools of water,
his tears stream down his ruddy cheeks.
I say hello through the sun.

I sit down in a white plastic chair.
I can see the backs of two prisoners.
One has a rectangle patch sewn
into his shaved head.
A little girl with crayoned hair
has her face pressed against the glass,
she is trying to talk to her Daddy.

We take turns talking on the phone,
until the guard behind us says,
"Visiting hours are over."
We say goodbye Dan.
This will be the way it is.
For 19 years.

We find the others in the baby room,
and give big teary hugs.
We leave prison,
and go out
into the dark,
cold,
Portland sky.

Jeannette Scheibe + ***Things You Do Alone***

Jelly stood poised with her hand over the sink, not seeing her face in the mirror, for what felt like a short time, but hours had passed. She wondered if it would hurt, she even said it out loud, to feel the words leave her lips, to hear her own voice, "I wonder if it will hurt." Nothing. No answer. No answer, of course, she was alone. The house was empty, maybe even the entire block. After all, this was the day of the big parade. That stupid fucking parade and everyone was going, but she wasn't. Not this time. She wasn't interested in standing in the hot sun waving a flag at a bunch of old farts in smelly uniforms. Why should she pretend to give a shit about what they did hundred years ago anyway? What did it have to do with today? Kids were dying everyday in far away places, in small towns, and for no good reason. No reason at all. Fuck it. Fuck all of them. The more she thought about it, the more pissed off she got. She wanted to get a bullhorn, go to the parade and scream, "You'll all wind up on a slab in the basement at some point! Naked and stiff, let's see how proud you look then!" But her words stayed in the room, floated around the walls and then left, unanswered. Jelly liked it, being alone that is, totally alone. There are some things you do, only, when you are totally alone. Like pick your nose, pop a zit, or take the perfect shit. That's what her brother Russell called it, 'the perfect shit.' Russell the asshole. He was such an asshole; it made jelly's head want to explode. He was always talking about masturbation and Internet porn when her friends came over, well, when her only friend, Margie Kleinsmith came over. Standing in her doorway (not really in her room, because he wasn't allowed in her room anymore), his stupid white sneakers just on the edge, just enough to make her crazy. Jelly's door was taken off a few months back, after the last big fight with her Mom, and Russell loved it. "I'm allowed to stand here, this is the hall! It's a free country!" Trying to provoke her. Jelly was powerless. Russell sneered at Jelly and smiled at Margie. His face covered in pimples, his teeth full of crap, he went on about something else foul. Margie stopped coming over after that. He was such an asshole; he was the president of the asshole club! And she knew there were clubs and groups for everything, even assholes. Gross. But Jelly never heard of a club for this, not for what she was going to do. This was something that had the true meaning of being alone. One time, she read about people trying to pair up or make a pact, she realized someone always had to be first and someone had to be last. The last person in the room. That's what she liked about it. She didn't want to share this with anyone. I guess I am selfish, she thought. Her Mom always said she was, and just last night when Jelly complained about her mom drinking too much, her mom said it again, "Jelly you're so selfish, this helps me, I'm not hurting anybody but myself! Why don't you think of anyone else for once?" Her mom had a glass of gin in one hand and a cigarette in the other, she got real close to Jelly's face when she said it, her eyes big and bloodshot, then she exhaled the smoke till Jelly coughed. Her mom smiled a wicked smile and stepped back. Better than a slap, Jelly thought. "Thanks a lot mom." Jelly said it softly and left the room before she said anything else. She didn't want to fight again. She didn't want to get hit. After a few minutes, she heard, "Ungrateful brat!" In the morning jelly knew her mother had drank until her bottle was empty and smoked until her ashtray was full. She didn't remember a thing. Just asked if Jelly was going to the parade with them and then smiled, that pathetic smile this time, the one Jelly hated even more. 'She's weak, I'm not,' Jelly thought. Then she screamed into the wall, as loud as she could, "I guess you were right mom, I am selfish! But I'm not hurting anybody but myself! I hope you're happy now!" Jelly looked at the razor in her hand, at the edge. She thought about a book she heard of, something about a snail balancing on a razor's edge? She didn't get. It didn't matter now anyway. She wouldn't read it. A cloud passed outside and a cool breeze broke through the window, 'Rain,' Jelly thought. Good. She smiled to herself at the idea of everyone running for cover, the old, disgusting men crowding under a awning so their old, disgusting uniforms didn't get wet. She especially liked the idea of Russell the asshole, and his new white sneakers getting covered in mud, it would make him nuts. Asshole. But the rain made her realize she had to hurry now. Her mother hated being out in the rain. It made her makeup smear and she hated that even more. There would be another fight. Jelly looked back into the mirror and she found a tear on her cheek, but didn't know why. Not looking down at the razor, she held it deep into her flesh, and than deeper still. She got her answer, it didn't hurt at all.

Whitney Walker + ***O'er Smasher***

The Oregon Territory throbbed on a forearm
as he kneaded fecal meat.
Thinning hide,
and lard slopped mane,
obscure the coarse lobes
rife with desire for good living.

Reaching deep
past the longing
for cartoon Saturdays
and safety,
grandstand fucking,
albatross whimsy,
and delusions of omnipotence.
I deny the pine
for the dubious mulligan,
the clean slate of youth.

Whitney Walker + ***Sidereal Punctures***

Winsome prayers cast for plumb terrain,
when and if only,
then life
will be worth living.
Then
I can
and will.

All that corrupt authority disdained,
crushed (the
soul) under it.

Hike the skirts of the past
to reveal
what's been when'd
and if'd.
One
wrestled,
the next
denied,
another
abstained.
All self,
afraid.

Mari Weiss + ***Dreaded Bees***

I got stung last night—didn't even see the sucker! One minute I'm moving some plants, the next I'm hopping around and swearing because of a sharp pain in my calf. I looked down and saw the stinger and I could not believe it. I hadn't been stung since I was a teenager when I stepped on a bee in my family's backyard. You see, I go to great lengths to avoid being stung. I am not a fan of bees. Oh, I appreciate what they do for us and the plane—all that lovely cross-pollinating not to mention being oh-so-helpful in explaining the ways of love —but even so, I prefer they keep their distance.

I'm much better than I used to be. Growing up I was terrified of them, which was tough because I loved the outdoors. Picnics and camping were just not fun what with all the jumping up and down and flailing I would do. God forbid one get in the car! I still can't believe I never put my car up on a guardrail. Well, actually I did put my car up on a guardrail but that had nothing to do with bees. I was a nut about them and that overwhelming terror was something I now know I learned from my mother. See, that was how she would react to bees—with such panic it was hard not to get caught up in her hysteria. She says she is allergic—or "deathly allergic" is her actual phrase—but she often uses that excuse for anything she doesn't like; like onions. She hates them and swears she is allergic but now we all know better having watched her eat pasta dishes with well-disguised onion in it. Even so, we, her loving family, indulge her by making special portions of onion-less guacamole, chili and other midwestern casseroles.

So when I stepped on that bee, oh so many years ago, and did not fall into anaphylactic shock, I realized I was not allergic. And that all those insane fears about being stung were—well, insane—because, truth be told, it didn't really hurt all that much. Last night's sting was more a shock than it was painful and I am reminded, one more time, that the dread and fear we have about pain and tragedy and even heartbreak is so often worse than the actual event. I have a friend who likes to say, "We terrorize ourselves on a daily basis." I hear ya, sister.

When I bought my first house I would lie awake at night, worried that there was something I was neglecting to do and it was just going to fall down on my head. Three and a half years later I have come to realize that if, after 75 years, an earthquake hasn't brought it down, what could I possibly do? I'm just not that powerful. I can't bring down a house and I can't stop bees from stinging. Oh thank god—now I can get on with my life.

Vicki Whicker + ***Hike the Skirts of the Past***

Puppies
Christmas
The homemade meals
The love and rockets that went off every New Year's Eve
Like clockwork
The way the socks were folded
And the way the beds were made, 1, 2, 3
4
After all that, turns out I made it all up

Turns out that dad had problems
Turns out that mom was never home to fix them
Turns out that it was not OK to hit me in front of my 3 brothers
That it was not OK for 1 brother to say, *she's not crying dad*, hit her again
Turns out that I ate more frozen pizza than a little girl should

Deepak Chopra can't help
Or the 4 Agreements
Father Martini tried and so did Sister Cocaine
But it's gone way past all that
Into the desperate corners that never get swept
Where the tears roll
And the tears collect

We wrestle and rub together, but it's not sex
It's tectonic plates and magma under the Andaman Sea
It's magnitude 9.1 on a stunning morning
It's arms and thighs desperate for rescue wrapped around a tree
He shoves me against the doorjamb
He is salvation; it's going to get rough
Into my brain, into the tempest, they come
Men with names, men with no names
Later, bruises bloom on arms and thighs
Futile prayers on the banks of the River Sangam
But with eyes closed, everything is blue
There is only this man
This moment
Por favor
Más profundo
En todo?
Si, Si, Si

Hike the mudslide hillside
Sleep in a cabin far from the useless aurora of LA
Where the Alpha Capricornids hoard their lights
While passé lover mugs my back, big bear
Reminds me of John and the time his head morphed into a reptile's
Pretty boy ugly lizard
I slept with him right then, no matter
I slept with hope and then hope again, no really
Hope that I did not see what I saw
Hope that I could not know what I knew
Hope that I would, somehow, get home alive

Hike the mountains on fire
Hike roughly the same path backwards
Hike through the dark and tangled woods
Markers of red skirt
Ripped from my stumbling
Grace the trail
I am bruised and bloodied, yes
But grateful, so grateful
I don't see the ocher eyes
I don't see the strips of meat
I don't see the taloned feet
Lord of the Way Home
Gorged full of my hope
Sees me

Stare
At the ceiling
Count the snores
Regret what I am at 1:57 in the morning
Forget the booze and the cigarettes
That fueled the quest
To find the right kind of man
Swimming through the blue-eyed haze
Of the Snake River Saloon
Pray for sleep
Hangover sunrise splinters fontanelle
Even the most ardent must eventually return to dust
I am tired, tired, tired
Close my eyes, see meteor showers
And even though I can tell by the way he breathes
That he is not my man
I stay

Hike
Until the fall-down
Learn
Winsome prayers fail
Fight
For plumb terrain

It used to be that whenever I thought of him
I curled into a ball on the shower floor
Let the hot water scald my memories
Repeated his name
Made my arms bleed
Bruised my thighs
Lost track of time
Let the phones ring
Like we used to do when we were
Counting the babies we'd have
Designing the houses we'd build
Fucking the meaning out of
I love you I love you I love you

It sounds like I am being held hostage by a barrage of pebbles
In some god-forsaken campground in North Carolina
It's been raining on our family reunion for 3 days
Turns out, cabins on the Yadkin River
With bug infested corners are a bad idea
But this is nothing compared with losing
The riverfront getaway pad that my mom used to own
The worst thing that had ever happened there
Was dad, checked out on the deck, vodka in his left hand
Cigarette trembling to ash in his right
Brothers cracking jokes at my expense
Sand in my hair
Worried by my fingertips, those
Tiny pebbles
Tiny asteroids
Tiny secrets
That fell and scattered into the folds
Of the blood-red couch that my mother bought
Back when she could own things
Back when she could make a good golf club sing
Back when her favorite blue heron slurped low-tide minnows
Along the fetid banks of the Cape Fear River
Back when she could breathe

Day 4, family reunion
I'm surrounded by flash flood warnings
I'm pounded by thunder thisclose
Bug bombed bugs lie in pieces everywhere
Mud and memories stick to the kitchen floor
Wet carpet stinks to the bottom of my guilt
It's just a week, It's just a week, It's just a week
I scratch the days off with a stick; I gouge them into the wall
Each raindrop's dead plop echoes against another's unanswered prayer
Mom's dead, Dad stole the car, Brothers won't stop, it's clear
The stork hit turbulence and delivered me to the wrong address

Stamens
Pollen
Unopened buds
Remind me again
Why I thought I was normal
To say yes to every man, drink, drug, thing
To push pedal to metal 110, 115, 120, just to see
To think that it was my god-given right to live every day
One bad idea closer
To the morning shower steam fetal curl

After all that, the truth is
There was no other way to go but to go through it
There is nothing left to do now but to slay dragons with rosebuds
And to say no
And to mean it

David J. Wilzig + ***Portugal***

Poems as places
build on the past
word upon word
rip-tiding through
memories
raising old thoughts
some jettisoned years ago
after dead relationship
others, flotsam lying
about, still intruding
banging about in one's head
oddly striking some
distant memory to
rekindle a lost
thought, a lost love.

The Algarve with
its white cliffs
could be Dover
but we didn't
honeymoon in Britain.
Perhaps the Celts
homesick for England
brought those rocks
to line the bay.

To write of Portugal
need I erase the
purple bougainvilleas, the
reddened begonias
surrounding sea-green tiles
laying on my hillside
miles from Dolly's place
and our hot summer days?

Bent over, pen in hand
hounded by the fear
of confessional banality
I search my mind
for the words
Auden directed of me
to learn from my
dreams what I lack.

I lack a menstrual calendar
but sperm can bear fruit,
proof I have five-fold.
Unafraid, I have slept
outside in the desert
eyes open to count star-sequins
sprinkled in the sky.
Yet, as a child
I feared the night
believing that the
curtains separating me
from outside blasts—
from bombs—
couldn't protect me
with the thinned weight
of a blackout shade.

Years from my honeymoon
the translucent turquoise seas
stretching out as far as
the Aegean
seen at another time with
these same eyes
and the sounds of birds
in the jacaranda and
the judas trees
unlike the East African drumming
of the Spice Islands
heard with these old ears
hair growing out
to be plucked as
the solitary hair
that lay unabashedly
beneath your nipple
as I nibbled.

Dreams of this young man
were experienced, kneaded
rolled and baked
as so many loaves

to be chewed
and digested with others.
Dolly's plates had three palms
Casa Tres Palmieras
her linen napkins
bleached white as Mikonos sails
hurt our eyes
with reflections of the sun
from the sea.
Her plates were blue and white
as sharply defined as
the Portuguese coastline
and so many
others I had
beached
on.

So you in your
red one-piece
black and white bathing suit
checkered bands
beneath your breasts and
beneath that area
you referenced
sighing
as the result
of your three children
sat across from me.
We two separated by a
sea of air
but seated in one craft
bobbing the waters
together.

Gulls overhead
blinding light
reflective shards of ocean
as daylight lightning bolts
seared my shielded eyelids
shocking my eyes upward
to search, to see
those snowy birds
with black tipped,
inkwell wings
prepared to write
upon the vivid blue sky
to tell the world
of dreams as yet
unrealized.

BOMBSHELTER PRESS

Anthologies

Twelve Los Angeles Poets (224 pp) $14.95

13 Los Angeles Poets (160 pp) $13.95

Moving Pictures: Nine Los Angeles Poets (62 pp) $5.00

Raising the Roof: Poets Supporting Habitat for Humanity, Riverside (72 pp) $10.00

The New Los Angeles Poets (203 pp) $12.50

Two-Women Show (Haft/Laumeister) (62 pp) $10.00

After I Fall (Alexander/Kulikov/Lee/Wilson) (64 pp) $8.95

Truth and Lies That Press for Life (216 pp) $12.95

4 Los Angeles Poets (ellen, Mima Pereira, Shirley Love, Anne Marple) (128 pp) $16.00

Books by Single Authors

Natural Selections (Elaine Mintzer) (120 pp) $16.00

A Lone Black Gull (Michael Andrews) (320 pp) $18.00

Coffin Lumber (Michael Andrews) (128 pp) $12.00

Breaking Down the Surface of the World (Jack Grapes) (62 pp) $10.00

Lucky Finds (Jack Grapes) (45 cards) $12.50

Chaos and Dancing Stars (Jean Katz) (140 pp) $15.95

Passion & Shadow (Judi Kaufman) (98 pp) $18.00

Crossing the Double Yellow Line (Stellasue Lee) (95 pp) $12.95

The Return of Sound (Zahava Sweet) (96 pp) $14.95

Corpses of Angels (Henry Morro) (72 pp) $12.95

ONTHEBUS

Double Issue 6/7 (330 pp.) $13.50
Charles Bukowski letters; interviews with David Mura & Joyce Carol Oates; provocative photo-essay by Penny Wolin, "The Jews of Wyoming."

Double Issue 8/9 (330 pp.) $13.50
Interviews with Allison Lurie, Anne Waldman, Thomas McGrath, Ai; color portfolio with poems by Pablo Picasso and surrealist paintings of his lover, Alicia Rahon.

Double Issue 10/11 (350 pp.) $13.50
Frida Kahlo full-color portrait & essay; last journals of Bukowski; interviews with Thylias Moss & Alice Notley; translations of Pablo Neruda.

Issue 12 (265 pp.) $11.00
Bukowski journals & photographs; interviews with Sharon Olds & Grace Paley; essay by Jack Grapes on the painting of F. Scott Hess.

Issue 13 (265 pp.) $11.00
Interviews with James Dickey & Tom Wolfe; Bukowski album of journals and poems.

Issue 14 (312 pp.) $11.00
Art by Susan Manders & Ruth Bavetta; Bukowski journals & poems; work by William Stafford, Ai, Donald Hall, Sam Hamill.

Double Issue 15/16 (324 pp) $15.00
Art by Ruth Bavetta & Susan Manders; Bukowski journals, letters, poems; interviews with Annie Dillard, Dorianne Laux, Kim Addonizio; drawings by Mindy Alper & Matt Wardell; work by Richard Jones, Lyn Lifshin, Ai, Suzanne Lummis, Katharine Harer, Kate Braverman, Charles H. Webb.

Double Issue 17/18 (332 pp) $15.00
Art by Susan Manders & James Doolin; Bukowski album; interviews with Arthur Miller, E. L. Doctorow, B. H. Fairchild; work by Katharine Harer, Lyn Lifshin, Suzanne Lummis, Doren Robbins, Bill Mohr, Kathleen de Azevedo, Henry Morro.

Double Issue 19/20 (288 pp) $15.00
Cover photo by Robert Durell; art by Aaron Smith; interview with John Irving; letters, journals, poems by Bukowski; translations of Yehuda Amichai, Gu Cheng,Táhirih, others; 20 reviews; writing by Steve Kowit, Richard Jones, Harry Northup, Michael C. Ford, Bill Mohr.

www.bombshelterpress.com
BOMBSHELTER PRESS
PO Box 481266 Bicentennial Station
Los Angeles CA 90048 USA

www.ingramcontent.com/pod-product-compliance
Lightning Source LLC
LaVergne TN
LVHW061224100826
845148LV00004B/851

* 9 7 8 0 9 4 1 0 1 7 7 9 4 *